CATHEDRALS OF THE WORLD

Text by

DAVID MOUNTFIELD

Crescent Books
New York

**Flyleaf: the vaults of Ulm Cathedral. Title page:
the spire of the Duomo, in Milan, and the statue
of the Madonnina. Center, an altar from the
cathedral in Mexico City. Top right, detail of the
façade of Rouen Cathedral.**

Designed and produced by
Editions Minerva SA

First English edition published by
Editions Minerva SA

ISBN: 0-517-365731

This edition is published
by Crescent Books,
distributed by Crown Publishers, Inc.

a b c d e f g h

©Editions Minerva SA
Genève, 1982

Printed in Italy

CATHEDRALS

"Cathedral" comes from a Greek word meaning "seat" or "throne", and a cathedral church ("cathedral" for short) is a church containing the throne of a bishop. It need not be a splendid church, and some cathedrals are quite humble buildings. Most, however, were built specially to serve as the chief church of the diocese, and tended to be larger and grander than the parish churches under the bishop's care.

The great age of stone-built cathedrals began in Europe in the 11th century and continued throughout the Middle Ages. Many new cathedrals have of course been built since then (some are still being built today), a few to serve new dioceses, others to replace buildings lost through war or other calamities. But essentially we think of a medieval—more particularly a Gothic—building.

The Gothic cathedrals of Europe are the finest artistic achievement of the Middle Ages or of any other period. Although we now know a great deal about how these divine dreams in stone were physically created, our first, simple reaction to them is one of sheer wonder at their technological virtuosity, quickly followed by a profound sense of spiritual awe. Historians and archaeologists may explain how technical problems were overcome, may describe the immense significance of the medieval Church and the permeation of thought by religious values, but however knowledgeable we become, in our spiritually impoverished age the great cathedrals are a kind of miracle, and their builders remain mysterious. As the 19th-century critic, John Ruskin, said of these often anonymous creators, "They have taken with them to the grave their powers, their honours and their errors; but they have left us their adoration."

In the 11th century, the style of architecture in Europe was what we know as Romanesque —in the Roman manner—of which the chief characteristic was the round arch. This form was employed not only for doors and windows but also for roofs: massive supports were needed to uphold barrel vaults, and windows had to be small to avoid weakening the walls. The structural drawbacks of Romanesque were largely overcome by the adoption of the pointed arch, the mark of the Gothic style (though not unknown in the Romanesque period), which greatly reduces outward stress. Vaults could higher, columns thinner, and huge windows of glorious stained glass could be inserted in the walls. Stone ribs carried the weight of the vault to certain points in the wall which were strengthened by buttresses. Eventually the flying buttress was developed to bridge a wider gap, making churches more spacious.

The Gothic style evolved in France, more precisely in the Ile de France around Paris. Some pedantic critics would say that it never really left, refusing the name Gothic (originally a term of contempt, incidentally, expressing disapproval of the departure from Classical conventions) to the medieval cathedrals of England, few of which can compare with the great buildings of the Ile de France in term of architectural purity. In any case, Gothic was nowhere a single style. We use the term of buildings from the 12th century to the 15th, and architecture did not stand still in that period. The Late Gothic or Flamboyant style of 15th-century France is very different from the Early Gothic of Laon or Paris.

The Gothic style is pre-eminently the style of northern Europe, where light was important and coolness unnecessary. It established such a hold on ecclesiastical architecture that the architects of later times found it hard to conceive of a cathedral in any other style. In the 19th century, when more new churches were built than at any other time since the Middle Ages, the majority of them followed —with varying authenticity— the Gothic style, and as late as 1948 a well-known ecclesiastical historian (D. H. S. Cranage) could write, "..the Gothic style... is still generally regarded as a necessity".   D.M.

INDEX

Above, sculpture over one of the side doors of Gloucester Cathedral. Right, the Door of the Savior, at Amiens: the Beau Dieu pier. Following pages, the rose window of Reims Cathedral.

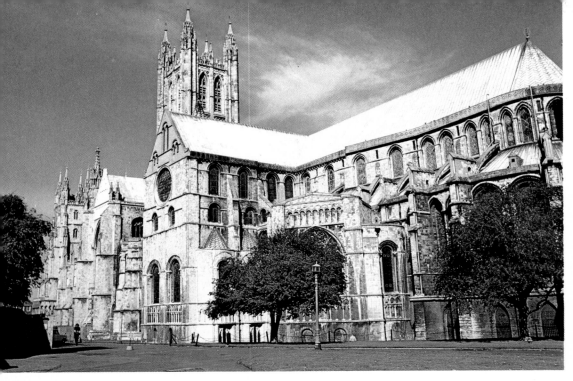

CANTERBURY

In 1161 Henry II, the most capable of English medieval monarchs, appointed as archbishop of Canterbury and head of the English–Church his chancellor and good friend Thomas Becket, hoping thereby to subordinate the Church to the Crown. Though usually an astute judge, Henry had made a serious miscalculation, for Becket promptly embraced the cause of the Church. For nearly a decade Church and State–archbishop and king–waged bitter conflict. Then four of Henry's knights, wrongly supposing the act would gain them royal favour, slaughtered the archbishop before the altar of his own cathedral.

The tomb of the martyr and saint became the most famous centre of pilgrimage in England. The King himself inaugurated the cult by walking barefoot to Canterbury, accepting scourging from the monks, and praying all night by the tomb. Guided by the gilded angel on top of the central spire, pilgrims in their thousands made the journey to Canterbury.

Today the steeple has gone and in its place is the Bell Harry Tower, the crowing feature of

The double-transept plan of Canterbury was to influence other English cathedrals, but the most remarkable feature of the building is its length, of the eastern part especially, which is nearly twice as long as the 60-metre nave. The latter is the work of a great 14th-century architect, Henry Yevele, and its slender piers and high arches make it one of the most spacious and distinguished interiors in the whole of medieval architecture. Despite this and other examples of the Perpendicular style, the dominant architectural image is of Norman and Early Gothic forms, created largely in the lovely warm stone imported from Caen in Normandy. Inside, Purbeck marble from Dorset was extensively employed, notably in the choir, transepts and Trinity Chapel where Becket's shrine stood. Thanks to Canterbury's unique position as premier English church and popular shrine, more of the medieval stained glass –some of it made in the same workshop as that of Chartres–has survived here than anywhere else in England. The windows of the Trinity Chapel, which depict the miracles associated with the cult of Becket, have successfully defied iconoclasts, 'improvers' and German bombs. Indeed, the old

Canterbury, built in the 1490s. The elegance of the tower does not, perhaps, quite match the general character of Canterbury, whose beauty is more rugged–in 18th-century terminology, sublime–than graceful. The cathedral incorporates the whole history of the Christian Church in England since the Pope sent St Augustine to convert the English in 547. There are no obvious traces of the original building, though the world of demons and monsters in the capitals of the crypt embody pre-Christian supersitions, and there are fragments of the early Norman Benedictine abbey.

and sacred associations of Canterbury, in the eastern part especially, inhibited the ecclesiastical authorities from the extensive rebuilding which, with their considerable revenue from pilgrims, they might otherwise have undertaken.

Canterbury Cathedral. The Archbishop of Canterbury is the head of the Anglican Church. Left, the exterior and tower; the interior seen from the altar. Above, ornamental detail of one of the vaults in the cloister. Right, the pulpit.

LONDON

The London church that most visitors probably know best is Westminster Abbey, the beautiful former Benedictine abbey opposite the Houses of Parliament, which was founded in 960, largely rebuilt a century later, and frequently altered or added to throughout the Middle Ages. While it illustrates practically every English style in that period—the famous fan-vaulted chapel of Henry VII standing as the culmination of medie-

Two views of Westminster Abbey (left and above), a building which occupies a central place in English history. Below, the dome of Saint Paul's Cathedral.

val English architecture—the church is, more than any other in England, predominantly French in character, and was partly based on Reims, the coronation church of the French kings as Westminster Abbey is the coronation church of the English kings.

The title of Westminster Cathedral belongs to the chief Roman Catholic church, a modern building in Byzantine style with a tower offering a splendid view of London.

The cathedral of London, however, is St Paul's, in the City. Old St Paul's was an enormous Gothic building, nearly 200 metres long with a spire (destroyed in 1561) 159 metres high. It was the most notable casualty of the Great Fire of London (1666), which destroyed most of the

medieval city, and its loss is still lamented. Little was saved except the monument to the poet Donne, for which he posed in a funeral shroud shortly before his death. However, the disastrous fire had some compensatory results. The hour produced the man, and that man was England's greatest architect, Sir Christopher Wren.

Wren, no admirer of Gothic, wanted to build a domed, Classical building, but the Church commissioners insisted on a cruciform plan. The resulting compromise, after two plans had been rejected, turned out a brilliant success (partly because Wren, with the King's connivance, altered the plans after they had been approved). The foundation stone was laid in 1673 and the building was completed in 1711, eight years before the architect's death at 91.

St Paul's is often compared with St Peter's Rome, to which it bears a superficial similarity, but it is, as one would expect, a more harmonious building. The division of the west façade into two tiers was a particularly happy stroke. The dome, with its supporting drum and gallery, is a masterpiece of elegant proportions, and the manner of its construction is a testimony to Wren's brilliance as an engineer and practical builder, in which, rather than in his designs, his greatest genius lay. The stone lantern is supported by an internal cone of brickwork independent of the outer and inner shells of the dome—an ingenious device.

The interior, airy, light and colourful, has choir stalls carved by a peerless artist in wood, Grinling Gibbons, and offers space for a vast congregation (for that reason it seemed more suitable for the royal wedding of 1981 than Westminster Abbey). In the huge, vaulted crypt lie the remains of the famous, military and naval heroes especially (also Wren himself). Great literary or artistic figures tend to find their way to Westminster Abbey. Most of us, no doubt, would be more than satisfied to take our final rest in either of these superlative churches.

London, St-Paul's: view from the altar; a grill; the floor of the central nave.

DURHAM

One benefit enjoyed by most English cathedrals (and denied to many French ones) is a splendid site. Durham cathedral stands high on a wooded, cliff-like peninsula skirted by the broad reaches of the River Wear, sharing is promontory with the bishop's palace and castle (now part of the university of Durham). Seen from the west, across the river, the three mighty towers of the cathedral convey an impression of massive invulnerability to which nearly one thousand years of history testify. Once they proclaimed the power of the Norman conquerors of England, and for centuries they served as a bulwark against raiding Scots from the north.

Durham is the finest example of the Anglo-Norman style of Romanesque, and for two rea-

Durham Cathedral, interior and exterior. Bottom left, the seal of John Wessington, in the annex to the sanctuary. (Wessington, a Durham prior of the 15th century, was an ancestor of Wahsington.) Ornemental motifs on a pillar.

sons: not only does it contain more Norman work unaltered by later generations, it is also the one Romanesque cathedral in England of truly remarkable design. It contains, in fact, all the main Gothic features—pointed arches, ribbed vaults (the earliest in Europe) and flying buttresses (hidden above the aisle vaults)—but remains essentially Norman in character and displays many of the features of English cathedrals.

The most famous relic of Durham is the body of St Cuthbert, saved from marauding Danes by the devoted monks of Lindisfarne and brought to Durham in 995. The White Church, built as a shrine, was pulled down by a Norman bishop who began the present building in 1093. The bulk of it was completed in the remarkably short time of forty years, though the Chapel of the Nine Altars, built around St Cuthbert's shrine, is a 13th-century addition and there are various other Gothic parts, such as the upper stages of the western towers, the transepts, cloisters and, of course, the triumphant 15th-century central tower. The unusual Galilee porch, a charming Early Gothic Lady Chapel, was built about 1170 at the

west end: a previous attempt to build it at the east end, as normal, had caused cracks, which were interpreted as St Cuthbert's way of saying he did not want ladies so near his resting place.

Perhaps unexpectedly, the interior of Durham is scarcely less impressive than the exterior. Great round columns, decorated with bold abstract patterns, march down the nave alternating with composite piers—each three metres in diameter. Among the furnishings are the Neville Screen carved in Caen stone with alabaster images.

The craftsmen of the Gothic age may have regarded the work of their Romanesque forbears as crude and primitive, and in a sense they were right. But such judgements seem strikingly irrelevant at Durham which, admittedly untypical and in advance of its time, is one of the outstanding buildings of the whole Middle Ages. Today it may seem strange to find such a building in what appears to be a remote corner of the continent, but in St Cuthbert's time the kingdom of Northumbria was probably the most civilized place in Europe, and Durham is a reminder of that heritage.

SALISBURY

Most great medieval cathedrals were inevitably built over a very long period, and betray the fact by the changing architectural styles manifest in their fabric. This is more evident in England than other countries: from one vantage point at Norwich one can see the work of at least seven centuries between the 11th and the 20th.

Salisbury is exceptional in that the bulk of the cathedral was built in a comparatively short time, between 1220 and 1258 in the so-called Early English period of the Gothic style. It is thus unusually "pure", architecturally speaking, and is characteristic of English Gothic in the same way as Amiens is of French.

A Norman cathedral existed in Old Sarum, a site which, despite its topographical eminence, did not commend itself to the bishops because of the close proximity of a royal castle and the difficulty in obtaining fresh water. In the early 13th century a new location was chosen on the level plain close to the River Avon (too close, as things turned out: the cathedral has been flooded more than once). The bishop laid the foundation stone—presumably not plundered, like some of the fabric, from the rejected Norman building—in 1220. Actually, he laid five stones, one for the Pope, one for the Archbishop of Canterbury, two for the Earl and Countess of Salisbury (or perhaps they laid their own) and one for himself. Thirty-eight years later, the cathedral was practically finished.

Salisbury is one of the largest cathedrals in England, slightly larger than Canterbury. Like Canterbury, it has double transepts and a prominent central steeple. The superb spire, at 123 metres much the tallest in England, was erected in the 14th century. The original builders had not counted on such weight, and extra buttresses were necessary; the wooden centering inside the spire was also left in place and can be seen there to this day. The west façade, not a total success and scarcely improved by 19th-century sculptures, was added about 1260, and the attractive octagonal chapter house slightly later.

Set in a wide expanse of rich green lawns, the cathedral can be seen from a great distance and, nearer to, the surrounding space augments the clean and graceful lines. The view from across the river is especially famous, thanks to the painter Constable.

On a dull, sunless day, the interior is less impressive. The proportions are fine, but one is conscious of an elegant stage without a play. The use of Purbeck marble for the columns makes a fine contrast with the predominant shade of pale grey of the stone used for the main fabric. But the stained-glass windows were destroyed during a misguided "restoration" undertaken in the late 18th century by James Wyatt, who knocked down the detached campanile to the north-west and removed two chapels. The monuments he placed in the nave are small compensation for these desecrations. In general, the 18th century "improvers" were far more of a menace than the Cromwellian troopers of the 17th century who, in practically all church guidebooks (which tend to be written by clergymen and therefore royalist sympathisers) are blamed for the destruction of medieval relics.

One should visit the cathedral on a bright day when a service is in progress and a joyful noise resounds through the nave.

In a quintessentially English setting: two views of Salisbury Cathedral and detail of the façade.

BRUSSELS AND ANVERS

There are no fundamental differences between the Gothic architecture of the Low Countries and that of the rest of Europe, though Gothic arrived comparatively late. The Brabantine Gothic style, which reached as far as 'S Hertogenbosch, derived mainly from France, but German influence was also important and the western façade of Ste Gudule, in Brussels, even has a faintly English appearance, probably a matter of coincidence rather than direct influence. Few Dutch or Flemish churches were built without a large and elaborate tower, the product of rivalry between the wealthy cities of the region, and there was also a tendency for churches to be relatively short. Antwerp cathedral, the finest example of the mature Brabantine style, built mainly between 1352 and 1411, typefies these tendencies. its magnificent north-western tower, topped by a three-stage lantern, rises to a height of about 122 metres, and the church is immensely wide (53 metres including six aisles), its total length of 118 metres being short by comparison.

Ste Gudule, whose church is known as the cathedral of Brussels, was a somewhat obscure saint who died in 712. Her life is illustrated in a triptych of the 16th century in the church which, standing on the slope of a hill formerly called Mont St Michel, claims St Michael as its second patron saint (he is, of course, also commemorated in Brussels by the gilded copper figure, three metres high, which graces the spire of the hôtel de

The spire of Antwerp Cathedral. The interior of the sanctuary... in the 17th century, as depicted in a Flemish painting (Prado). Right, façade above the side door. Far right, Brussels Cathedral and the Pulpit of Truth (in the Jesuit style).

ville in the Grand-Place). Ste Gudule was founded in 1220, after the previous church had been destroyed by fire, and the choir is one of the earliest examples of Gothic in the Low Countries: the apse, in fact, strongly suggests lingering Romanesque influence. The church was a very long time under construction, and it has also been extensively renovated at various times since which, together with the mixture of influences it incorporates, makes it architecturally rather complicated. The general plan of abbreviated transepts without aisles and wide chapels flanking the choir on north and south, is typical of the Low Countries. The nave, with its circular columns (matching those of the choir) which support statues of the apostles, was built in the 15th century. The carved foliage on the capitals is characteristic Brabantine work, and the unusual pulpit of carved oak, illustrating the Fall, is said to have been a gift from Maria Theresa. The glass of Ste Gudule, which is famous, includes portraits of other Habsburg notabilities, such as the Regent Mary, sister of the Emperor Charles V and widow of Louis of Hungary (killed at Mohács in 1526). The large window at the west end (16th century, but restored in the 19th) displays an extraordinary number of figures at the Last Judgment, and in the north transept and adjoining chapel a rather grisly little anecdote of 14th-century anti-Semitism is related in fine colours.

AMIENS

If one had to choose a single building to stand for all the great cathedrals of France, the cathedral of Amiens would be a strong candidate. Not only is it the largest (large enough to hold the whole medieval population of about 10,000 people), it represents the peak of the High Gothic style of the 13th century.

Since the Middle Ages the centre of the city has moved, and the cathedral is no longer at its heart. Reconstruction has made it difficult to envisage its original situation, though as one approaches through the narrow streets to the south-east, the cathedral springs dramatically into view, a perfectly proportioned (though the original spire was about fifteen metres taller) vision of slender but steely vertical forms. Our modern architects often manage to make a building of glass and slim girders look heavy; the builders of Amiens contrived to make stone look as light as air. Even the glass of the windows is held in place by a minimum of tracery, and the flying buttresses allow the pigeons free flight through their ascending arcades. As an example of economy in the use of material, the cathedral of Amiens would make an excellent study.

The foundation stone was laid in 1220 by Bishop Evrard de Fouilloy, whose bronze tomb can be seen in the nave, and the master mason primarily responsible for the plan and superintendent of the work for nearly thirty years, was Robert de Luzarches. Clearly he had the example of Reims (begun nine years earlier) in mind, though Amiens is a slenderer building, its walls comparatively thin and its main columns rising in slim, uninterrupted shafts to support a vault higher than any in France except Beauvais.

Unusually, constructions began at the west end, so that the existing church of St Firmin, in the east, could be used until the latest possible moment. The present cathedral was, in fact, the fourth church to stand on the site; its immediate predecessor was destroyed by fire in 1218. Again, though less disastrously, fire broke out in 1258, damaging the uncompleted choir and transepts, but the main work was complete by 1269, when in solemn cerumony, attended by the future King Edward I of England, the precious remains of St Firmin were transferred to their new and grander home.

By that time the famous figure of the Vierge Dorée was probably in her place on the door to the south transept. She is frankly portrayed as a contemporary lady of fashion—the soubrette of Amiens, Ruskin called her—with three carved angels who are adjusting her halo to the most becoming angle. Though no longer 'golden' (the statue was originally gilded), she remains a figure of irresistible charm.

Fortunately, nearly all the sculpture has survived quite well, and although much of the overall effect of Amiens depends on precision, ligthness and lack of clutter, the sculpture is rich and hardly excelled anywhere. The west façade, though structurally less impressive, is a perfect encyclopedia of the beliefs and teaching of the 13th-century Church, while the calm assurance and perfect purity of the building seem to be finally concentrated in the serene, welcoming figure of the Beau Dieu at the west door.

Amiens Cathedral: the rose window, the organ and the façade. The construction of this masterpiece of Gothic art was begun in 1220.

BEAUVAIS

Like the soul of man, the builders of the great Gothic cathedrals aspired to heaven: verticality, upward movement, these are the hallmarks of the pure Gothic style in France. Naturally, it was not spiritual aspirations alone that raised the walls higher and higher until the soaring vault, seen from the ground, seemed to float in the firmament. Among the prosperous, expanding towns of royal France, all classes of citizens combined in their determination to outshine their rivals. Each new cathedral had to be larger or grander than its neighbours. In particular, the height of the vault steadily increased. Laon, begun in 1160, first set the record. Paris, begun 1163, exceeded it. Chartres, 1194, added another metre or so and Reims, 1211, topped that. Then Amiens, 1220, leaped nearly five metres higher, with its vault raised nearly 43 metres above the floor.

At Beauvais, on the edge of the Ile de France, the medieval builders reached the limit. The choir of the Cathedral of St Pierre rose to an incredible height of 47.95 metres. A building of fourteen or fifteen floors could have been erected in the choir without touching the vault. In terms of sheer daring, this is the outstanding achievement of medieval French architecture.

The citizens of Beauvais did not enjoy their triumph for long. In 1284, only twelve years after the choir was built, the walls began to bend outwards. The roof groaned and sagged, and fell with a crash to the floor below.

That disaster (by no means unique) did not end the ambitions of Beauvais. Nearly three centuries later, a huge spire was erected, despite the fact that the nave had not yet been finished because the money for it had been used to repair the choir—strengthened by additional piers. For a few years the lofty spire held its own; then, without support from the west, it suddenly collapsed. Once more, the choir had to be rebuilt.

The cathedral was never finished. The transepts were built in the early 16th century, with all the lavishness of the Flamboyant or Late Gothic style evident on the south façade, but the

central tower was never replaced and the little Romanesque church of the Basse-Œuvre still occupies the site destined for the nave of the cathedral. Otherwise, apart from some fine stained glass by a local artist in the Renaissance period (augmenting the rich medieval windows) and the addition of a complicated astronomical clock in the 19th century, little has been done to the cathedral. A massive and splendid block, held together internally by iron rods and externally by huge, three-tier buttresses, it stands today as a memorial to the high ambitions of its builders. In modern eyes this crippled giant, like Michelangelo's unfinished sculptures, is perhaps a more splendid sight than the completed building might have been.

The Cathedral of Saint-Pierre, Beauvais—a most unusual piece of ecclesiastical architecture, in that it has no spire. The fineness of its vaulted ceilings and the beauty of its stained-glass windows are thus emphasized.

ROUEN

The old Norman city of Rouen, seat of an archbishop since the 4th century, was for a long time the largest city in France outside Paris. The size and splendour of the cathedral of Notre Dame mirrors the historical importance of Rouen, while reminding us also of its often violent past: conflicts between English and French, revolts against the Crown, war between Catholics and Protestants, depredations of bandits in the post-Revolutionary era, and the bomb damage of 1944.

Rouen was a great centre of art in France in the 15th century and one of the first places to reflect the ideas of the Renaissance. An outstanding example of Renaissance art can be seen in the memorial to the two cardinals d'Amboise, in black and white marble eight metres high, which is situated in the early 14th-century Lady Chapel, the most exquisite part of the building with windows surmounted by lofty openwork gables.

Although archaeological research is best conducted by other means, it is true that the high explosives with which so many cities have been visited in this century, besides causing death and destruction on a horrific scale, have also led to interesting discoveries. At Rouen, for example, bombs revealed evidence of a very early church, built about the end of the Romano-Gallic period. The present cathedral dates from 1202, the previous building, like so many others, having been damaged by fire. Some parts, like the base of the dignified Tour St Romain, are earlier, and others much later. Most of the immense west front and the other western tower, the Tour de Beurre, are Late Gothic. The cost of building the Tour de Beurre was raised by sale of dispensations allowing butter to be eaten during the Lenten fast; hence its name.

A spire was regarded as an essential part of a cathedral in the Middle Ages, and the fact that comparatively few cathedrals in France or England have one can be ascribed to the vulnerability of such structures, or to a lack of cash. The mighty spire of Rouen, topping the central tower and rising 156 metres (the highest in France) is actually made of cast iron and is, of course, a 19th-century creation, erected to replace the spire destroyed by lightening in 1822. Critics regard it as disproportionately high, and there is no doubt that the cynic who compared the unusual top of the spire to a candle extinguisher struck on an apposite, if unfortunate image. Indeed, Rouen cathedral impresses with the beauty of its parts rather than the coherence of the whole. The west, with its flanking towers which make it so immensely wide, is one of the finest examples of the Flamboyant, while the choir and chevet have a noble simplicity. But perhaps the most intriguing approach is by the northern Portail des Libraires, past the buildings of the quaint Cours des Libraires where, in the 14th century, shopkeepers displayed their wares.

Rouen: the cathedral towering over the town and the surrounding area (top right); the façade (left). Right, the famous Butter Tower, so named because the patterns on its stonework resemble those made in butter; Rouen is the capital of Normandy, a noted dairy-farming area.

PARIS

The cathedral of Notre Dame in Paris is one of the most familiar buildings in the world, rivalled only by the Eiffel Tower as a popular symbol of the French capital. The stones of Notre Dame have witnessed great historic events, and few churches have suffered more indignities from the hand of man.

Like all medieval cathedrals, it was the centre of city life as well as a house of God (at Chartres, there was an employment exchange in the transept). The homeless used the cathedral as a hostel, hunted men sought sanctuary, knights took the Crusader's oath, travellers displayed ostrich eggs and stuffed crocodiles. Market stalls clustered around the walls and the famous minstrels of Notre Dame entertained the populace. Here King Henry VI of England was crowned king of France at the age of ten.

Disastrous alterations were made in the 18th century by those who had no sympathy for the Gothic; the stalls were destroyed, the columns clad in marble slabs, and the precious stained glass knocked out of some of the windows to give more light. The worst came from the excesses of the Revolutionary era, when the holy cathedral was declared a 'temple of reason' and an actress was crowned Goddess of Reason on the high altar. Incredibly, the cathedral was auctioned for building stone. Napoleon came to power in time to prevent it being knocked down and in 1804 he was crowned emperor in Notre Dame, the lavish scene being splendidly recorded by J.-L. David, who was not in the least inhibited by the fact that he was elsewhere at the time.

That the cathedral survives in its present state seems remarkable, and a great debt of gratitude is due to that prodigious architect and

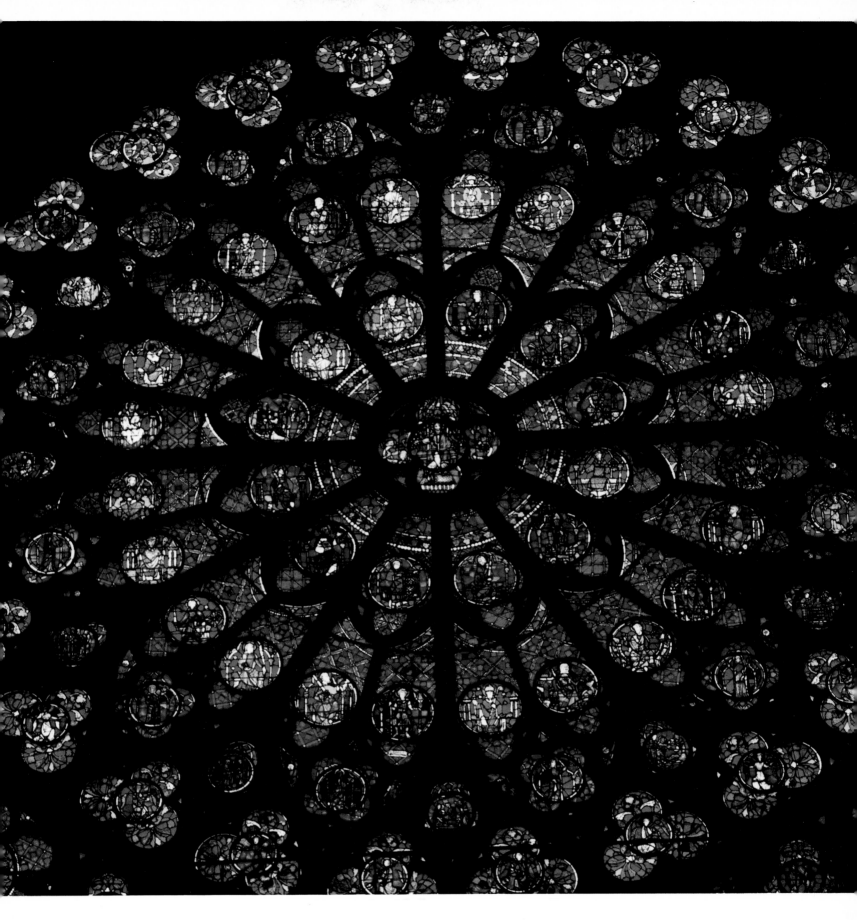

scholar, Viollet-le-Duc (1814-79), who supervised the retoration of so many great Gothic buildings. Even the famous gargoyles are his work, and although not everything that Viollet-le-Duc did is universally admired, there can be no doubt of the value of his restoration of the great cathedral of Paris, where he had wandered as a boy. (The rose

The nave and three familiar views of the Cathedral of Notre-Dame de Paris, which has been intimately involved in all phases of French history. Above, the stained glass of the rose window.

windows, he recollected, reminded him of the huge flowers of a funeral wreath, sad and resplendent, which seemed to break into song when the organ began to play.)

Notre Dame of Paris was begun in 1163 and at the time it surpassed all other cathedrals, owing much to the conception of the remarkable Bishop Maurice de Sully, born a wood-gatherer's son. A double-aisled plan was adopted, creating a series of soaring, shifting vistas within and, outside, compelling the double leap of the magnificent array of flying buttresses. Standing on an island in the Seine, the cathedral seen from the

east appears as a great oared vessel sailing resolutely towards her harbour—an image that struck medieval theologians no less forcibly than it does us.

The other main aspect is from the west, where the powerful, squarish façade, growing steadily lighter in texture as the eye moves upward from the portals to the towers, proclaims the resilience and refinement of medieval French culture. The towers of Notre Dame may not dance, as the saying goes, but that is not their purpose. Viewed from the west, the cathedral presents a perfect image of nobility and strength.

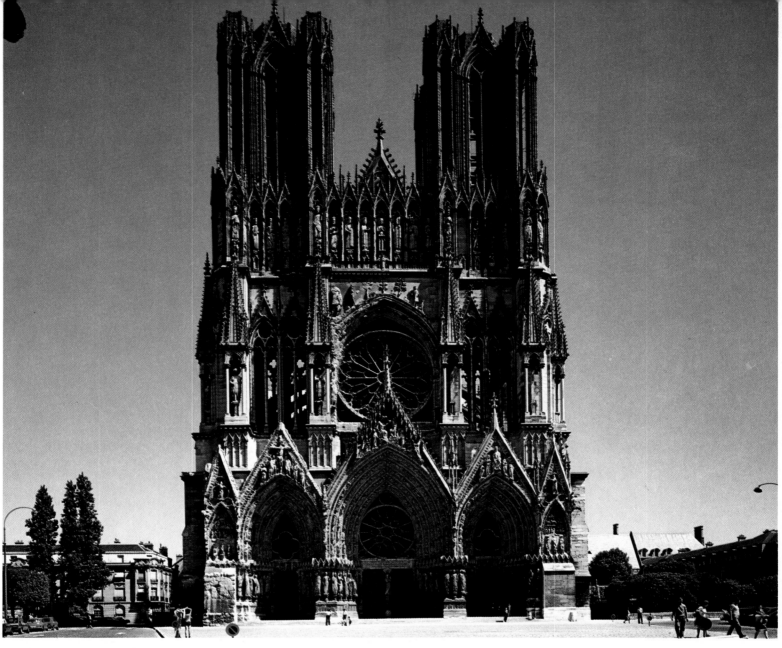

REIMS

The city of Reims is very old, but even its most loyal citizen would hesitate to call it beautiful. The medieval city has almost disappeared under the weight of modern industry, though the cathedral has benefitted from the clearing away of some of the buildings that used to huddle against it.

It was at Reims that Clovis, the ancestor of French kings, adopted Christianity nearly fifteen centuries ago, and later the kings of France were crowned in Reims cathedral. Their statues can be seen decorating the west end of the building, together with the scene of Clovis being annointed with the holy oil which descended with the dew from heaven.

The present cathedral was begun after the old one was ruined by fire in about 1200. At first construction proceeded swiftly, but the relations between the archbishop and the people were often cantankerous, debts piled up, prompting the Pope to urge the clergy to greater effort, and the struggles of French and English armies during the Hundred Years' War caused further delays. Nevertheless the cathedral, apart from the upper towers, was finished before the end of the 14th century. Charles VI ordered that stone might be collected for the towers from any territory within a distance of four leagues, including planted fiels and orchards. By 1427 the towers were completed, and two years later Charles VII was annointed king in Reims cathedral in the presence of the person to whom he owed his kingdom—Jeanne d'Arc. Today the cathedral has a slightly battered appearance, partly the result of damage during the First World War, when it received several direct hits from artillery shells.

Fittingly for its royal role, Reims is perhaps the grandest cathedral in France, and a classic specimen of the High Gothic style. Majesty is proclaimed from every aspect, but especially by the magnificent west façade. The decorative details are immensely rich yet unusually uniform—especially remarkable considering the long period of construction. Although crowded with sculpture, it is not cluttered: there is always a sense of space, a logical relationship between different units, and the sculpture never contradicts the architecture. It is at Reims, above all, that one is reminded of Emile Mâle's view of the sculptures

of the great French cathedrals as 'mirrors of God'.

There were Roman remains in the area and it is obvious that the sculptors of Reims were well acquainted with Classical models: one has only to look at the frieze of figures rising from the dead (some of them, indeed, rising from antique urns rather than Gothic coffins) to reject the notion that Gothic artists could not portray a convincing human nude. The larger, standing, draped figures include some of the most famous examples of medieval sculpture. The angel in the scene of the Annunciation is a figure typical of Reims but almost unique in the art of the period in that the face wears a smile which is genuinely benign—not the usual ghastly Gothic grin. A new spirit of naturalism can be seen at work in the sculpture of Reims, where Classical balance, pagan identification with nature, and Christian charity, are beautifully combined. Apart from the figures, the decorative foliage is carved with striking fidelity: at least thirty different kinds of plant have been identified. Hours and days could be spent studying the sculpture of Reims (and lamenting the poor state of some of it). Even then there would be more details to discover, like the figures of two peasants harvesting grapes, lovingly wrought against a background of vines, on the capital of a column in the nave.

The imposing Reims Cathedral, where the kings of France used to be crowned, and two details of the porch. Above, the *Smiling Angel,* one of the statues of the façade, which is often presented as portraying the French spirit.

CHARTRES

Chartres has become the most powerful symbol of the French Gothic age; the name alone sums up an image of the Middle Ages which, though its relation to reality may be doubtful, has a strong appeal for the modern mind. This appeal is hard to recapture in words or even in pictures.

At the first, superficial glance, Chartres is not spectacular; stately, yes, but approaching from the west, the portals look a little cramped and to an unfamiliar eye the unmatched spires strike a slightly dissonant note. Closer acquain-

tance banishes criticism. The southern tower, with its assured proportions and its brilliant switch, at roof height, from square to octagonal, has been declared to be one of the greatest architectural achievements of all time. The later, northern spire is an equally assured example of the Flamboyant style and now, after five centuries of close association, appears the ideal companion to the southern spire.

Chartres is, in fact, the first truly Gothic cathedral. The chunky form of the flying buttresses, characteristic of the general geometry of Chartres, suggest Romanesque influence but,

more important, they were built—for the first time —as an integral part of the structure. The quadripartite vaulting was also new, and set a pattern for High Gothic churches everywhere.

Though built swiftly in a burst of civic enthusiasm (all but the transepts were completed in a single generation by 1220), this is a highly sophisticated building. The master mason based his elevation on the Golden Section of antiquity, and measurements reveal that the height of the shafts corresponds exactly to the breadth of the nave between the columns. There is a sense of divine equilibrium.

In the Middle Ages Chartres was not only a famous centre of pilgrimage—its most famous relic being the Virgin's shift presented by Charles the Bold in 876—it was also the greatest centre of learning and culture in northern France outside Paris. The cathedral is an enduring testimony to the northern humanist tradition, which is displayed is the beautiful sculpture—extraordinarily well preserved—and above all in the stained glass.

Medieval people were fond of comparing the windows of Chartres to jewels, and the comparison still seems apt. The earliest windows date from before the fire of 1194 which necessitated the rebuilding of the cathedral. Not only do they represent some of the finest glass ever made,

they are pleasingly simple to understand—not always the case with medieval stained glass. The dominant colour is a mystical blue, the precise shade of which modern technology has been unable to emulate. The famous glass of Notre Dame de la Belle Verrière, with its smouldering reds and heavenly blues, belongs also to the 12th century, though the window itself is later. Most of the rest of the glass belongs to the 13th century and it is indisputably the finest collection anywhere. It reaches a climax in the rose windows—the Last Judgement in the west front and in the south transept, and in the north transept the truly gem-like rose dedicated to the Virgin, which is accompanied by lancets with superb figures from the Old Testament.

Even the finest photography cannot convey the beauty of stained glass and Chartres, still a centre of pilgrimage today though for different reasons, is a cathedral that must be visited.

Chartres Cathedral is visited by more people than any other building in France. Note, in particular, the angel carrying the sundial, at one of the corners of the cathedral. The stained glass is among the most famous in the world. The two windows reproduced here depict the epic of Roland and Charlemagne (13th century).

BOURGES

It has been said that, seen from a certain point to the south, the great cathedral of Bourges has an almost log-like character. Unusually, it lacks transepts; the uninterrupted sides of the building do have a slightly monotonous appearance, scarcely relieved by the short south tower at the western end.

Structural problems account for some of the unusual features of the Cathedral of St Etienne. The impressive crypt, for instance, is largely the result of a need to compensate for the unevenness of the site, and the chequered history of the twin towers suggests insufficiently strong foundations. The dwarfish south tower, slightly divorced from the main building and buttressed by a curious structure called the *pilier butant*, was never completed nor hung with bells because of fears that it would sink. The northern tower dates from the early 16th century, the original tower having collapsed in 1506.

Bourges has close affinities with Paris. Its founder, Henri de Sully (archbishop 1182-99), was the brother of the archbishop of Paris, currently completing Notre Dame. Significantly, the transepts of Notre Dame, though present, are rudimentary; at Bourges this tendency was carried to its logical conclusion. There are other similarities, both in plan and in details like the choir screen.

The west façade, though something of an architectural jumble—from Romanesque to Flam-

boyant—and still bearing the scars of the 16th-century religious wars, is the most impressive exterior aspect, gaunt but magnificent. Its tremendous width hints at the most extraordinary feature of Bourges, which becomes breathtakingly apparent when one steps inside. A constant problem in large medieval buildings was the achievement of breadth. The pointed arch and the flying buttress made it possible to create a more spacious interior than the Romanesque style permitted, but the fact remained that while the length could be continued almost indefinitely, as in many English cathedrals, and the height could be raised to extraordinary levels, as in northern France, the width of the building was limited. Various attempts were made to overcome the difficulty. One thinks of the bold, 22-metre vault of Gerona in Spain or the hall churches of Germany. At Bourges, by essentially orthodox means, a great airy hall was created—a single spatial unit almost without parallel in Gothic architecture. As at Paris, there are double aisles, but at Bourges there are no galleries and

the inner aisles rise to the unprecedented height of 21 metres, thus solving the problem of light which afflicts Paris. The supporting piers are identical throughout nave and aisles and rise in clean, uninterrupted lines, seeming slenderer than they are, towards the lofty vault. The nave actually widens slightly towards the east—a fact unnoticed by the human eye, the limitations of which this device is designed to overcome by preventing the normal optical illusion that parallel verticals converge.

Bourges has other glories. Its 13th-century windows are second only to those at Chartres; some of its sculpture—particularly the Last Judgement in the usual position above the west door—is comparable with that of Reims. But it is that marvellously integrated interior space that the visitor to Bourges always remembers.

Bourges Cathedral: rose window and portal; the columns; and the cathedral seen from the southeast.

Early in the 13th century the Church decided to crush the Albigensian heretics once and for all. The Pope preached a crusade, and a ferocious war began, more savage than the Crusades against the Saracens, which ended the independence of the great princes of the south and all but destroyed the brilliant Provençal civilization. At Albi, Toulouse and other places, the remorseless Inquisition consigned hundreds to the flames; gradually all heresy was ground into extinction. After the counts had lost their estates, the bishop was made the chief temporal authority at Albi.

The fires were still smouldering when Bishop Bernard de Castanet began the building of the Cathedral of Ste Cecile in 1282. With moat and wall to defend the bishop's castle to the north-east, the new cathedral took on the appearance of a fortress rather than a church. "For the people of Albi", as someone remarked in the 15th century, "never lived at peace with their lord". The main building was finished in about one hundred years, a monolithic block of brickwork, red like the soil of the country or the blood of the slaughtered, with semicircular attached towers supporting the walls and the powerful western tower (completed later). No ornament relieved the outward appearance of uncompromising strength. A few later pinnacles and the large and over-adorned porch added in Late Gothic times, together with a well-meant 19th-century addition of an ornamental frieze running along the top of the walls, topped by a balustrade, merely serve to emphasise the austerity of the rest.

But Albi is a building of extraordinary contrasts, and inside the impression is quite different. In the extraordinarily wide and spacious interior, well-lit by the bright sunlight despite the narrowness of the windows, the dominant colours are pale blue and gold. This is the work of the Renaissance. In the early 16th century the whole interior was frescoed by an Italian painter of great ability. His work is known here and here only. One might think he had little time for any other work, but in fact his task at Albi was completed in only six years.

But the most remarkable of all the sharp contrasts Albi presents is to be found in the east, where there is what amounts to a church within a church, similar in proportions but in visual effect quite different. The choir is a jewel-like filigree of white stone, of unsurpassed richness and refinement even in the Late Gothic period, when craftsmen took such delight in delicate workmanship. The first reaction of Cardinal Richelieu, it is said, was suspicion that the work was painted plaster, and he would not believe it was stone until he had subjected a sample to close inspection.

The last contrast offered by Albi is that of two styles so different in the same country and the same period as this fortress-church, representing the south and the contemporary monuments of northern France.

In Languedoc, in the south of France, the Cathedral of Sainte-Cécile, Albi, with a view from the bank of the Tarn. Following pages: the central vaulting of Beauvais and Amiens cathedrals.

MÜNSTER

Münster was once the capital of Westphalia, and though long eclipsed in terms of population and wealth by places like Dortmund and the cities of the Rühr, it still remains the spiritual capital. Now as in medieval times in the Cathedral Square of Münster on market day, the stalls are packed with the good things of which the people of Westphalia are so fond. The air is heavy with the smell of sausages and cheap cigars. The cathedral, broad and firmly rooted in the soil, forms a natural backdrop for the lively scene. It is neither so large nor so elegant as many others, but despite the extensive reconstruction necessary in the aftermath of war, its deep golden stone has an air of permanence, and the building has a study character all its own.

The cathedral is seldom empty of worshippers, who come for perhaps a few minutes private prayer, or to pay respects to the tomb of Cardinal Galen, stalwart opponent of Naziism. The chapel next to the cloisters, still possessing a fine Romanesque tympanum, is often used for private prayer, while those who enter through the south door find more to admire in the Gothic statues of the porch, where scenes of Paradise are represented.

According to a survey carried out some years ago, the people of Münster are still more religious than most; at least, they go to church in greater numbers. In the past, religion in Münster could take extreme forms: for this was the city of the Anabaptists.

At the time of the Reformation, Münster held a position of some independence from its powerful bishop, with whom the citizens were customarily quarrelling. Lutherans dominated the council and when two Anabaptists missionaries arrived from the Netherlands, they were made unexpectedly welcome. Münster, they decided, was the New Jerusalem, and under the leadership of Jan Bockelson of Leyden they proceeded to rid the city of unbelievers. Those who resisted were killed or driven into the snow. Private property was abolished, and all books except the Bible were burned. Some of the statues of the cathedral were despoiled; it is amazing that any survived, such was the violence of Anabaptist mob rule. Since there was a superfluity of women in Münster, a haven for apostate nuns, Bockelson also intrduced the practice of polygamy. His fanatical discipline and terror tactics kept the bishop at bay for a surprisingly long time but, under siege, the city began to run out of food. It fell at last to the combined forces of the Catholic bishop and the Lutheran landgrave of Hesse, whose troops made bloodily certain that Anabaptists would cause no more trouble in Münster. (The instruments of torture used on the Anabaptists can be seen in the museum today.) The city reverted to the old religion, and it remains today a predominantly Catholic city in a largely Protestant region.

Three views of the imposing Munster Cathedral, in the heart of Westphalia.

COLOGNE

Cologne cathedral is the largest Gothic church in northern Europe. Standing in a flat landscape in the centre of the city, it is an imposing structure, in some obvious respects one of the most awe-inspiring of European buildings. But for the majority of people it has never commanded the same admiration that is lavished on many less impressive structures. This may be partly due to the unusual proportions, and it may have something to do with political sympathies.

The floor covers about 8,454 square metres and the width is great compared to length (84: 142 metres). The nave is almost as high as Beauvais, and the two western towers, 156 metres high, are of massive proportions—so massive that in spite of the great overall width there is no room for a large central window. Judged by strict conventions, the proportions of Cologne are far from ideal, and the intricate decoration of the steeples is a little monotonous in effect. Inside, the discrepancy in height between nave and aisles seems abrupt, but one is soon diverted from these considerations of overall form by the treasures the cathedral contains, most notably the shrine of the Three Kings, containing the relics which made

this a great centre of pilgrimage in the Middle Age.

Cologne was one of the wealthiest cities in Europe in medieval times, its archbishop a powerful prince and one of the seven imperial electors. When the construction of the present cathedral began in 1248, Cologne was a place of civic violence; relations between citizens and archbishop were frequently hostile and their quarrels were often savage. It would have been surprising if the cathedral had been successfully completed, and in fact little more than the choir was built in 200 years; a stationary crane sat on the stump of the south tower for over a century. During the Napoleonic wars, the building was used as a barn and a military prison.

The grim events of those years provoked a wave of nationalist reaction in which the cathedral was at last to rise as its medieval planners

Cologne Cathedral is one of the high points of German sacred architecture. Above, right: a striking juxtaposition of Gothic and modern architecture. Bottom, left to right: the Altar of the Virgin (14th century); a 12th-century reliquary; the ring of a door, depicting Jonah and the whale.

intended. The citizens were urged to complete it 'as thanks to God for the liberation of the fatherland from French bondage'; Goethe, Schlegel and the future Friedrich Wilhelm III rallied to the cause. A special tax was levied to pay for the work and, miraculously, the original plans for the west end were discovered. Some 400 people were employed on the job for nearly half a century, and by 1880 it was finished. The massive steeples rose to proclaim the growing pride of the new German nation. Badly damaged during the Second World War, the cathedral has been restored once more, and it remains a symbol of political aspirations.

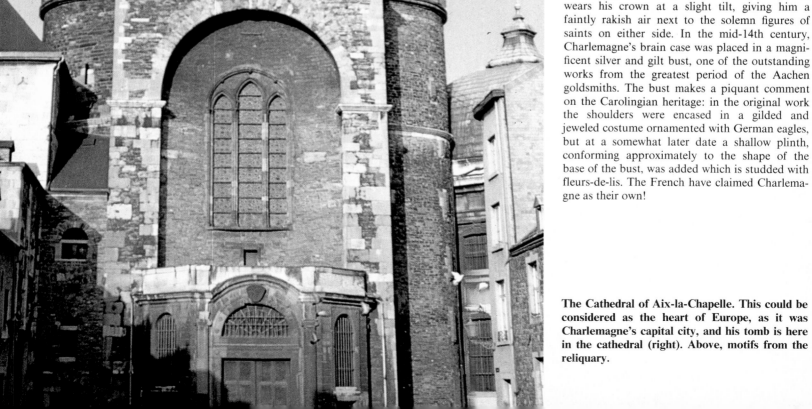

When Charlemagne selected Aachen (Aix-la-Chapelle) as his capital in the late 8th century, he was planning a rival to such great centres as Rome, Ravenna (both of which he had visited) and Byzantium. To Aachen, then, came men like the scholar-statesman Einhard and the Yorkshire-man Alcuin, who played a leading role in the Carolingian revival of art and learning, as well as Italians, Greeks, Provençals, Jews and Arabs. To Aachen came the scribes who transcribed texts in the Carolingian minuscule style (our knowledge of many Roman works is due solely to them), the builders, goldsmiths and other craftsmen—the finest in the continent. There too Charlemagne built his shrine, the future enthroning church of the German emperors, dedicated to Our Lady by the Pope in 805. The simple throne of marble slabs on which Charlemagne sat and later medieval emperors were crowned is still in the gallery, facing the altar.

The church took the form of an octagon with projecting apse, and it has usually been assumed that it was modelled on the Church of San Vitale in Ravenna, though Professor Jean Lassus and others have pointed out that the plan, with its emphasis on strength rather than subtlety, belongs more to Roman than Byzantine tradition. Whatever its source, however, it is certainly the finest surviving example of Carolingian architecture.

Inside the octagon, with its three tiers of arches and marble-columned arcades, the building still appears much as Charlemagne saw it, but otherwise it has been greatly altered over the centuries. A soaring Gothic choir replaced the Carolingian apse in the late 14th century; the tall outer roof of the octagon was added in the 17th century, and the western steeple was rebuilt in 1884. There are also subsidiary chapels of the late Gothic period.

Charlemagne endowed his church with many relics and sacred objects. Some of the glories of the Carolingian era, as well as later medieval artefacts, are kept in that remarkable repository, the cathedral treasury. The Charlemagne shrine, to which the sainted Emperor's remains were transferred in the early 13th century, is a magnificent object in gilded silver and copper with coloured enamels and gemstones. Charlemagne, holding the church in his hand, wears his crown at a slight tilt, giving him a faintly rakish air next to the solemn figures of saints on either side. In the mid-14th century, Charlemagne's brain case was placed in a magnificent silver and gilt bust, one of the outstanding works from the greatest period of the Aachen goldsmiths. The bust makes a piquant comment on the Carolingian heritage: in the original work the shoulders were encased in a gilded and jeweled costume ornamented with German eagles, but at a somewhat later date a shallow plinth, conforming approximately to the shape of the base of the bust, was added which is studded with fleurs-de-lis. The French have claimed Charlemagne as their own!

The Cathedral of Aix-la-Chapelle. This could be considered as the heart of Europe, as it was Charlemagne's capital city, and his tomb is here in the cathedral (right). Above, motifs from the reliquary.

Mainz is one of the oldest cities in Germany. Its strategic importance at the confluence of the rivers Main and Rhine was recognised by the Romans, and the Roman town became the capital of Germania Superior. Though frequently ravaged during the *Völkerwanderung,* it was an early centre of Christianity: from Mainz St Boniface set out in the 8th century to convert the pagans, and the archbishop of Mainz became the primate of the Church in Germany. During the Middle Ages *goldene Mainz* (gilded Mainz) was an immensely prosperous imperial city with a population almost as large as it is today. The grand old cathedral stands as witness to the power and magnificence of the Salian dynasty and, in particular, to the energy of the Emperor Henry IV as a builder of cathedrals, though his work in this respect probably owed more to his desire to check the political ambitions of the papacy than to personal piety.

The three great Romanesque cathedrals of the Rhineland, Mainz, Speyer and Worms, from a closely associated group, partly for geographical reasons, of course: it is possible to see them all in one day, although a less hectic schedule is preferable. They have obvious affinities. All three are primarily constructed of the same red sandstone from local quarries, and though Worms was begun one hundred years later, all are of approximately the same period, typifying the Romanesque style and demonstrating why that style was less easily displaced by the Gothic than in other parts of Europe (the west end of Mainz was built in the 13th-century but in the same style as the late 11th-century east end), and why it is even possible, when looking at these buildings, to feel a certain romantic regret that the Gothic style was ever invented.

Mainz is the most spacious and perhaps the grandest of the three, as befitted the seat of the powerful archbishop of Mainz, though paradoxically its grandeur is partly due to Gothic or proto-Gothic features and to later restorations. There is, for example, a decided emphasis on the west front with its twin towers, usually considered a characteristic of Gothic cathedrals, and the Gothic parts of the handsome polygonal towers are certainly desirable additions.

The cathedral has a remarkably chequered history. "Alas Mainz", the cry that greeted the death of Henry IV in 1106, might have been uttered in many another crisis. The *basilica nova* built by archbishop Wiligis was apparently burnt down on the very day of its dedication in 1009, rebuilt at once but again completely destroyed in 1081, resulting in the building of the present cathedral under the auspices of Henry IV, with the conscious intention of surpassing the cathedral of Speyer, under construction during the same period. Thereafter, work was inhibited by further fires, interspersed with an earthquake and a hurricane, although these alone do not explain the frequent complaints about the state of the building. As elsewhere, shortage of cash, constitutional quarrels and urban riots played their parts. In the later Middle Ages Mainz entered a long decline, and Napoleon was sufficiently shocked by the state of the cathedral to order a major restoration.

Two views of Mainz Cathedral.

WORMS

In the *Niebelungenlied* King Gunther and Queen Brunhilde hold their court at Worms (the name is popularly supposed to be connected with the German *Wurm,* a dragon, and has no connection with the humble English earth-worm). The destruction of the city by the Huns in 436 was also the basis of heroic legends. Rebuilt by the Merovingians, Worms was an episcopal see in the 7th century, if not earlier, and the site of a palace where Charlemagne stayed and his daughter Emma, according to legend, was courted by Einhard. The power of the bishop of Worms

steadily increased, especially under Burchard I, who founded the cathedral in the 11th century. Eventually, the citizens gained a certain independence from their unloved rulers and Worms became an imperial city, a favorite meeting place of the imperial diet. Here, momentously, Luther took his stand before the Emperor Charles V in 1521, and a few years later the city declared itself for the new doctrine, suffering disastrously as a result during the Thirty Years' War. Today, however, the cathedral of Worms belongs to the Roman Catholic Church.

There is an atmosphere of calm reassurance about the tall and imposing cathedral of

St Peter and St Paul, a peace and quiet not unconnected with the fact that Worms is a rather less bustling place today than it was in the Middle Ages, despite its generally modern appearance.

The Romanesque style in Germany, of which Worms, together with its Rhineland neighbours Mainz and Speyer, is a noble example, lasted longer than it did in other parts of Europe, persisting in some places well into the 13th century. Worms cathedral is essentially a simple building, following the characteristic plan with an apse at each end, which rules out the possibility of a grand western façade, as in French cathedrals, and results in the main entrances being placed

north and south instead of west. Built of a deep red sandstone and generally somewhat reticent in ornament, Worms has a special dignity, its tall, cliff-like walls and solid piers ascending into Romanesque shadows. The original building was consecrated in 1110, but little remains of it except the lower parts of the western towers and the general plan. The remainder was mostly comple-

Worms, the scene of the famous Diet in 1521, has a fine cathedral (above). Left, Saint Martin's Door; the saint is shown on Dorseback. Bottom, interesting detail of an architectural motif on one of the towers.

ted before the end of the 12th century, but the vault dates from the 13th century and the elaborate south portal was added in the 14th. Some other parts, including the fine central octagon, have been rebuilt at various later times. There are two octagons, crowned with pointed roofs, and a fine pair of towers at each end, which reinforce the pleasing impression of uniformity. The picturesque doubling-up of elements—apses, towers and octagons—derives from Carolingian tradition (it can be seen in the Carolingian abbey of St Gall), but the influence of North Italian architects appears in the vaulting and the arcades of the octagon.

The Gothic style in Germany evolved in very different ways from that of France. The Germans developed a passion for tall spires, and it became common to build one giant steeple instead of two at the west end. Ulm minster is the prime example, towering 161 metres above the ground, the tallest in Germany. To reduce weight, the builders employed elaborate tracery and open-work: as one gazes up at the steeple of Ulm the sky can be seen in the spaces between the stone, making the gigantic structure comparatively light and graceful.

The German *Sondergotik* ("special Go-thic") is partly due to the rise of individual artist-craftsmen whom we know by name and by their work on individual buildings. Very often, dynas-ties of masons can be traced all over Europe, one famous example being the Parler family, who worked on the choir at Ulm. Ulrich von Ensingen belonged to another well-known family. He be-came the master mason at Ulm in 1392, redes-igning the nave and planning the great western tower. Though a comparatively young man, he already had a considerable reputation. Today he is best remembered for his work at Ulm, but at different times he was engaged at Strasbourg and at Milan, where, not surprisingly, he soon quarrel-led with his Italian colleagues whose architectural ideas differed markedly from his.

Ulm minster had been founded fifteen years earlier in a burst of patriotism which followed a decisive victory over neighbouring Würtemberg and was accompanied by a rapid rise in the prosperity of the city. Ulm, the city of the *Meistersinger*, had been a free imperial city since 1155, responsible to no one but the Emperor, and the citizens spared no expense on the construction and decoration of their church, which was to be large enough to hold 30,000 people. That figure was probably larger than the contemporary popu-lation, though by the late 15th century, when Ulm was the leader of the Swabian league, the popula-tion was about 60,000 (larger than the census of 1905) and its territory covered nearly 800 square kilometres.

The great success of the medieval city notwithstanding, the monumental bourgeois church was not completed. Ulrich von Ensingen's tower, of which he built only the first stage, caused technical problems and was considerably altered. The spire was not built until the 19th century, albeit to the old plans. At that time also the roof was strengthened with iron, but these additions were too much for the old brick walls to bear and the present flying buttresses, which march with military precision along the flanks of the nave (reminding one observer of a guard of honour accompanying a catafalque) were also built.

It cannot be said that the overall design, however impressive, is entirely ideal. The interior is something of a disappointment, but there are some wonderful works of art, sculpture (especially the strikingly realistic Christ as Man of Sorrows on the central pillar of the porch, dating from about 1430), paintings, and of course wood-carvings, perhaps the most remarkable feature of Gothic art in Germany.

Ulm Cathedral: overall view. Its tower is said to be the tallest church tower in the world; the left side of the nave; the baptismal font; the main door.

MUNICH

The bombs of the Second World War ensured that contemporary Munich is a markedly different place from the fabled Bavarian capital of old. Roughly one-third of the buildings were destroyed, including old churches and palaces, the famous Wittelsbach Residence and several museums, though the large and ugly quarters of the Nazi party were unscathed. The Frauenkirche, Church of Our Lady (patron saint of Munich), also survived, though not entirely unmarked. Valuable objects had been removed and gafely stored, though the richly carved choir stalls, dating from the late 15th century, were badly damaged. Fortunatetly, some of the half-length figures by Erasmus Grasser (about 1502) from the back of the stalls escaped. The church itself, a cathedral since 1817, today shows little sign of the disasters of the 1940s and in fact some of the losses to the interior were suffered at an earlier period; it cannot be said that the 19th-century

restoration was entirely well-judged, and stern critics would also deplore the additions made about the beginning of the 17th century.

As one sits, flagon in hand, and contemplates the familiar brickwork of the Frauenkirche, as much a symbol of the city as Notre Dame is of Paris or Westminster Abbey is of London, one is conscious of certain vague contradictions. For a start, it is hard to explain exactly why the building looks so much at home where it is, in a city comparatively "modern" by Bavarian standards (it originated in a famous act of vandalism by Henry the Lion, who in 1158 destroyed the bridge and profitable market of the bishop of Freising and built another bridge and another market slightly upstream, whence the profits were diverted to himself). Admittedly, Munich is not a city

Munich Cathedral with its distinctive towers is a symbol of Catholic Bavaria. Above, one of the modern stained-glass windows. Right, the monument to King Louis of Bavaria, who reigned during the first half of the 14th century.

dominated by a particular style or period, like Romanesque Regensburg, but is rather a collection of different kinds of buildings, much of their magnificence due to the enthusiasms of Ludwig of Bavaria. The Frauenkirche, however, is a distinctly austere building in this city of beer drinking and merrymaking, and it is one of the few genuinely indigenous buildings of Munich. It is of the Bavarian hall church type (creating a spacious interior but potentially dull exterior), and was built in the 15th century by a local architect of no previous reputation, Jörg von Halsbach, known as Ganghofer, who turned out to be extremely competent if not inspired. Construction was complete, except for the towers, by 1479, when the vast job of constructing the roof (140 rafts loaded with timber were required for the roof frame) had been successfully completed.

The towers suggest another slight contradiction. Like the rest of the building they are, though large, comparatively unpretentious and simple, yet they have more character than many more ambitious structures. Perhaps this is another example of the effect of familiar association. The profile of these towers has over the centuries assumed a symbolic character.

At Ratisbon (Regensburg), on the site of an earlier Celtic settlement, the Romans made a base from which they commanded the upper Danube valley. Later the city became the first seat of the dukes of Bavaria, and the centre from which Christianity spread throughout southern Germany. There was an abbey here in the 7th century, and the bishopric was founded by St Boniface a century later. The first cathedral existed as early as 778, but is was replaced by a Romanesque building in the 11th century, the appearance of which can be calculated quite accurately as a result of archaeological excavations in the 1920s. Some parts of it survive, of which the most appealing are St Stephen's Chapel and All Saints' Chapel, a little octogonal tower with projecting, semicircular apses decorated with 12th-century murals in a remarkably good state of repair.

In 1273 the Romanesque cathedral was so badly damaged by fire that it had to be rebuilt. Regensburg then was at the height of its prosperity. It had recently acquired the status of a free imperial city, and much of the rich produce of Venice and the East still travelled across its famous bridge on the Danube. The prospect of building a new cathedral was therefore one that could be entertained with equanimity.

Construction began in 1275, folowing the familiar ground plan but introducing the High Gothic style of Strasbourg. The east end of the cathedral was virtually finished in half a century, but after that progress slowed down. Regensburg's greatest days were over, and although it would be famous again as a seat of the imperial diet and as the headquarters of the princes of Thurn and Taxis, Europe's first 'postmasters-general', it was suffering from competition with other Bavarian cities, like Augsburg and Nuremberg. Money was running short. However, the nave, with its large clerestory windows that practically fill each bay, was built according to plan, the western towers were built up to the top of the gable in the 14th century, and the façade in the 15th. About 1530 building came to a complete stop. Although the original plans were incomplete, the cathedral might have been a more interesting example of German Gothic without the addition in the 19th century of the crocketed spires, which are in the conventional manner and tend to detract from the unique charm of the façade, with its exquisite little triangular porch and highly individual sculpture. But, seen from across the Danube, the spires certainly make the silhouette more impressive.

The interior of the church was refashioned in the Baroque style in the late 17th century, but King Ludwig I, the self-appointed artistic mentor of Europe, condemned this embellishment of the pure Gothic and had all traces removed in the 1830s. The interior therefore has a slightly austere appearance, especially by Bavarian standards, despite the presence of some fine sculpture and stained glass.

Regensburg Cathedral (bottom left) is adorned with some superb Gothic motifs such as this *Dance around the Golden Calf* (center) and the splendid couple shown here, but its altar (top left) is pure baroque.

VIENNA

Although Vienna is an ancient city, it is not a place where one expects to find many medieval buildings; nor, with due respect, are its citizens renowned for godliness and piety. Yet there is the Stefansdom, the cathedral church of St Stephen, a mighty edifice in the very centre of old Vienna, its great steeple marking the hub of the city like a gigantic dart.

The church (it did not become a cathedral until later) owes its origin to Ottokar the Great of Bohemia, who held the duchy of Austria between 1251 and 1276, and though not much of the present building existed at the latter date, it can be truthfully said that St Stephen's existed before Vienna became the Habsburg's city.

Nearly all ancient cathedrals were built, added to, restored or reconstructed at various times, but as a rule the combination of different styles achieves a certain harmony and the differences may not be immediately apparent. Judged by purely architectural standards, which is really no adequate way to judge any medieval catehdral, St Stephen's is an ill-assorted building. It is packed with beautiful things of every period from the Romanesque to the 19th century, but the many hands who contributed in successive ages appear to have worked with scant awareness of

bank or an insurance company, are 19th-century work. This type of construction, ruling out a clerestory, makes for dimness within, but there is light enough to admire the rich Baroque decoration, the splendid tomb of the Emperor Frederick III, and the Late Gothic pulpit carved from a single block of stone by Anton Pilgram, whose self-portrait can be seen below the pulpit steps.

The west front, with its great door and unusual little octagonal towers, is the oldest part, incorporating some of the previous, Romanesque church. The transepts serve as entrance porches, and above the south transept rises the splendid steeple, 137 metres high, which was raised during the first third of the 15th century (an intended twin, on the north transept, was never built). One of the most splendid spires in the whole of German Gothic architecture, it is unusual in the relative absence of openwork, the effect of heaviness being instead combated by the intricate modelling and crockets.

A discriminating visitor once remarked that to appreciate the cathedral of Vienna, at least from the outside, one must largely abandon architectural for humane standards.

St. Stephen's Cathedral, in the heart of Vienna; the spire, the organ, baroque decoration of the choir, and the splendid pattern of the roof.

their predecessors' intentions.

Basically, Vienna is a 'hall church' of the characteristic German Gothic type, in which there is no decisive differentiation in height between nave and aisles; all three are, in Vienna, of about the same width also. An immense, steeply sloping roof covers the whole in a single span. The distinctive tiled zig-zag pattern of the roof, and the huge Habsburg eagle that sprawls across the adjoinning choir like a billboard advertising a

MILAN

Though one of the earliest appearances of the pointed arch was in Sicily, that was due to the influence of the East on the island's Norman rulers: the Gothic style in architecture never took firm root in Italy. Unlike France, Italy had no central monarchy with the capacity to pursue consistent policies over many generations; Italians tended to remain loyal to the Classical tradition of which they were the heirs, and the Gothic style for ecclesiastical buildings had fewer advantages in the south than it had in northern Europe.

There are, however, exceptions. While the South languished under Spanish rule and Rome stagnated during the exile of the popes in Avignon, an "Italian Gothic" style was adopted in

Few buildings deserve to be described as 'stone lacework' as fully as the Duomo, in Milan. Left, scene from medieval history depicted in bronze on the portal.

the North. Structurally, it really depended more on Romanesque tradition, but Tuscan and Lombard architects recognised one great advantage of the Gothic, its achievement of interior space. Both Florence and Pisa are examples of a new spaciousness. In some places, quite individual styles evolved, the two most significant being Venice and Milan.

Started in the late 14th century, Milan cathedral was the largest building project of its time. It was supported by all classes of the population from the dukes downwards, and paid for by the sale of indugencies and similar stratagems. On occasion, when money ran short, unskilled labour was provided gratis by the citizens. But despite all these efforts, the cathedral took a long time. The façade was only begun in the 17th century, the 15th-century lantern had to wait until the 18th century for its spire, and the north side was not completed until the 19th century. There are still a few unfinished details.

Although the influence of the Gothic style of France is plainly evident, Milan is really an example of the basic lack of sympathy for that style in Italy. Many of the attributes of the High Gothic are present: flying buttresses, enormous

windows, and a perfect forest of pinnacles. But there is a very un-Gothic emphasis on horizontals; the roof is low-pitched and the building has none of the soaring effect of trans-Alpine Gothic. During its construction many experts from northern Europe were invited to advise on the technical problems, but most of them stayed only a short time and departed with feelings of frustration, if not outrage. For all its Gothic appurtenances, it remains a characteristically North Italian structure, based on sophisticated geometrical design with the elevation built up of a series of equilateral triangles — a concept wholly alien to the masters of the northern Gothic.

Built of brick faced with pinkish marble, Milan cathedral is one of the most remarkable buildings in Europe. Its great bulk is offset by the incredibly complicated exterior decoration. The lantern is an engineering triumph and the polygonal apse, with its elaborate windows, is a masterpiece. The building contains a lesson in the history of sculpture from the 14th to the 19th century, though the lofty interior is generally austere. The final result of five centuries of construction is a tribute to the ambitions of the old duchy of Milan.

VENICE

Venice is like no other city in Europe, and the cathedral of San Marco is like no other church. For many centuries the Serene Republic was the greatest power in the eastern Mediterranean; it largely controlled the luxury trade with the East on which its prosperity grew, and its citizens looked not towards Rome but towards Byzantium. Secure on their islands, the Venetians successfully defied the Franks, and remained loyal to the Eastern Emperor, an allegiance formally recognised by Charlemagne in 810. Despite occasional setbacks, Venice retained its pivotal position between East and West throughout the Middle Ages.

The first doge built the first church of San Marco as a chapel attached to his palace in the 9th century; he organised the retrieval of the body of St Mark, patron saint of the republic, from Alexandria and installed it in the church, where it remains. The present building, begun in 1042, is the third on the site and incorporates part of the 10th-century basilica which replaced the original, wooden building. It is unique in European architecture for two main reasons. It was profoundly influenced by the East, especially by the lost Church of the Apostles in Constantinople, and many Byzantines worked on its construction, along with craftsmen from Lombardy, evolving a style of architecture peculiar to Venice. Secondly, no European church can equal the richness of San Marco's ornamentation.

The basic plan is of a Greek cross, with a central dome and smaller domes over each of the four arms; the western half is enclosed by a narthex, or portico, which makes the building almost square in plan. The glittering façade includes elements from many lands, brilliantly coloured stone and marble, transparent alabaster and sparkling mosaics, allegorical sculptures, bronze horses from the Arch of Nero, gilded cupolas of wood and delicate, fretted pinnacles, arches and niches added in the Late Gothic period. Above rise the domes, glistening under the blue sky. Seen from the great open space of the Piazza San Marco (the ballroom of Europe, as Napoleon called it), the total effect is at once lavish and yet, notwithstanding the mixture of ingredients, a perfectly satisfying whole. To the right rises the splendid Romanesque campanile. Despite earthquakes and subsidence, the Venetians were fond of bell towers and this one lasted until the early years of this century before it collapsed (it was restored with commendable fidelity).

The interior is no less rich. The brilliance of the gold backed mosaics, mostly completed by the 14th century but some designed by artists like Titian and Veronese, relate stories from the Bible. There are well over 4,000 square metres of glass mosaic covering the available areas of walls, arches and domes — not counting the baptistery and subsidiary chapels.

In the late 12th century Venetian merchants returning from overseas were obliged to bring some treasure home for San Marco. Today Venice is less wealthy and the state of the city causes international concern. But so far San Marco has survived, remarkably, intact.

St. Mark's Basilica, Venice : in an exquisite city, a dazzling piece of architecture, whose interior is matched only by its façade. Bottom left, the sculptural group known as the 'Four Kings'.

PISA

The complex of buildings south of the Campo Santo in Pisa form one of the most attractive architectural vistas in Italy, and in spite of the fact that they were constructed over a period of more than 200 years, they display a pleasing stylistic conformity.

According to tradition, the cathedral of Santa Maria Maggiore was begun by the thankful citizens of the maritime republic in gratitude for a naval victory of 1063; but in this case, as in many others, scholarly research has cast a shadow of doubt on legend by asserting that work was not begun until about 1089.

The cathedral is a basilican church in the form of a Latin cross, expanded in size during the course of construction but without spoiling the original plan. From the outside the most impressive view is from the west, where tiers of arcades rise one above the other. Classical as well as Lombard and Byzantine influence is apparent; inside the cathedral the view towards the east is dominated by the immense mosaic of the Redeemer in the apse.

The baptistery, begun over a century later, is a circular building, the inner space being about twenty metres in diameter between the columns. Its original appearance was obscured by Gothic additions in the 14th century, the one blot on the perfection of Pisan Romanesque which, otherwise, the whole complex displays.

Schoolchildren throught the world who may have only the haziest idea where Italy is or what the Christian religion means are invariably familiar with that uniquely fascinating structure, the campanile, better known as the "Leaning Tower of Pisa". This eight-storey circular tower, perhaps the most beautiful Romanesque tower in southern Europe, is at present tilted about five metres from the vertical. It looks as if it is about to fall over, and as the tilt is apparently increasing at a constant rate, it will undoubtedly do so: engineers can predict the year it will happen unless, as one assumes (though not with total confidence), something is done to support it. The tower is not, of course, supposed to lean, though at one time some people believed it was. Begun in 1174, it was only half built when, towards the end of the 13th century, the anxious citizens observed that subsidence had caused it to tilt. Giovanni Pisano was called in but whatever he advised, the problem was not solved. Nevertheless, construction continued: the belfry was not installed until 1350. It would now be unthinkable, even if possible, to straighten it. The Leaning Tower is too firmly imprinted on the popular imagination. However, it is now leaning quite far enough!

The Leaning Tower of Pisa is situated in the same group of buildings as the cathedral (above). In the foreground, the Baptistry, the upper part of which is reproduced at bottom left. Right, the pulpit, by Pisano.

FLORENCE

The great Gothic cathedrals of northern Europe were erected by largely anonymous craftsmen. In Italy, individuals were better known, and the names of those who contributed to Santa Maria del Fiore, the cathedral of Florence, reads like a roll call of the great artists of the early Renaissance, from Giotto to Michelangelo. The cathedral consists of several units, the campanile, the nave, the octagon with its famous dome, and the baptistery; most of it was constructed between 1296 and 1462.

The interior is surprisingly plain and tranquil, not the overflowing treasury of masterpieces one might anticipate. It does contain wonderful works of art, notably the unfinished Pietà of Michelangelo, abandoned in pieces by the artist but reassembled by a pupil, and there are marvellous details, like the frieze of dancing children in white marble by Donatello. Only the marbled floor echoes the brilliantly decorative exterior, with its panels of coloured marble and small ornamental windows.

In 1296 the old church of S Reparata was deemed no longer worthy of so properous a city, and Arnolfo di Cambio was appointed to build a new one. The original plan is therefore his, though it was expanded during the 14th century when Giotto, Andrea Pisano and Francesco Talenti were successive masters of the works. The campanile was designed by Giotto, though only the first stage was built in his lifetime and his original scheme included a spire. The baptistery, to the west, is the oldest building of the group and was probably once a church in itself. Its most famous features, apart from the dome, are the bronze doors, the south door by Pisano in the 14th century and the others by Ghiberti a century later. Ther latter, which feature in practically every modern book on the Italian Renaissance, were the winning design in a competition, with Brunelleschi among the unsuccessful entrants.

The crowning glory of Florence is of course Brunelleschi's dome, one of the most discussed and most influential structures in the history of architecture. The dome, however, is unique. Brunelleschi had studied antique buildings in Rome, including the Pantheon, but the pointed and ribbed dome of Florence is contructed bascially on Gothic principles. The octagon on which it rests could not be changed, and the architect's contemporaries doubted if his project were possible, since he had to span nearly 43 metres. But Brunelleschi built his dome — strictly two domes since there is an inner and outer shell — without (it is said) timber centering and without exterior buttressing. Instead, he bound in the base with timber and iron rods, employing tension to prevent the dome splitting outwards. The work began in 1420 and took over 14 years.

Florence Cathedral has the dignified bearing of a huge ship in the midst of the hills of Tuscany (right). The plain yet rich beauty of the choir (bottom) is quite as remarkable as the inlaid marble of the baptistry or the façade (left), the portal or the splendid font (below).

ROME

Whether or not it is true that this is the place where St Peter was buried, and archaeological evidence suggests that it is, the site of the basilica of St Peter has been revered since the earliest Christian times. The great building which stands there now, the headquarters of the Roman Catholic Church and possibly the largest church in the world, had its origin in the ambitions of Pope Julius II, one of those Renaissance popes whom it is easier to imagine in the hunting field (or battlefield) than in the pulpit, though he was an overpowering personality in either place. His plan was to demolish the old basilica and replace it with a magnificent new shrine to proclaim the eternal verity of the Christian faith and the power and magnificence of the papacy.

The competition to find a worthy architect was won by Bramante, whose basic design took the form of a Greek cross with a dome, inspired by the Pantheon, mounted on a colonnaded drum. Work began in 1506, but in 1513 Julius died and Bramante was replaced. Several famous artists were subsequently associated with the work, including (briefly) Raphael, who proposed a plan in the form of a Latin cross. By his death in 1520 funds were running short, and in 1527 Rome was sacked by the Protestant soldiers of the Emperor's army, an outrage that shocked Europe and, for a time, checked the building of St Peter's. In 1546

Michelangelo was appointed to supervise the project. This incomparable genius was then over seventy; nevertheless, the outstanding features of St Peter's are largely due to him. He returned to the Greek-cross plan and designed the great dome, completed after his death in 1564. Early in the 17th century Carlo Maderna lengthened the nave and built the gigantic façade, which hides the dome from view in some part of the piazza, and finally, Bernini, that prince of Italian Baroque, created the spacious piazza with its elegant curved colonnades in the 1650s and 1660s.

St Peter's is more than a building, however splendid, and the whole great Vatican complex of which it is the main feature arouses feelings that vary according to the personal allegiance of the individual: it is difficult to treat St Peter's as simply a church or, indeed, a museum.

The exterior, which is not easy to comprehend as a unit, offers little guidance to what lies within. There appears then to be not one but several churches, and the atmosphere changes as one passes from one part to another. Under the soaring dome one is possessed by a feeling of lightness and delicacy, and in the wide central nave, the dimensions of the building permit Baroque decoration which might seem too ornate in a lesser building. There are, of course, magnificent works of art — Michelangelo's Pietà, one of the best-loved sculptures of the world, and Bernini's brilliant throne of St Peter, in the apse, which uses light as a sculptural element.

The Pope has his seat not in St Peter's but in the basilica of St John Lateran, a much older church but so greatly altered over the centuries that very little of its 10th-century origins are visible.

St. Peter's, Rome, heart of Catholicism. Its magnificence of design was clearly intended to express both the spiritual authority and the temporal power of the papacy in the 16th century.

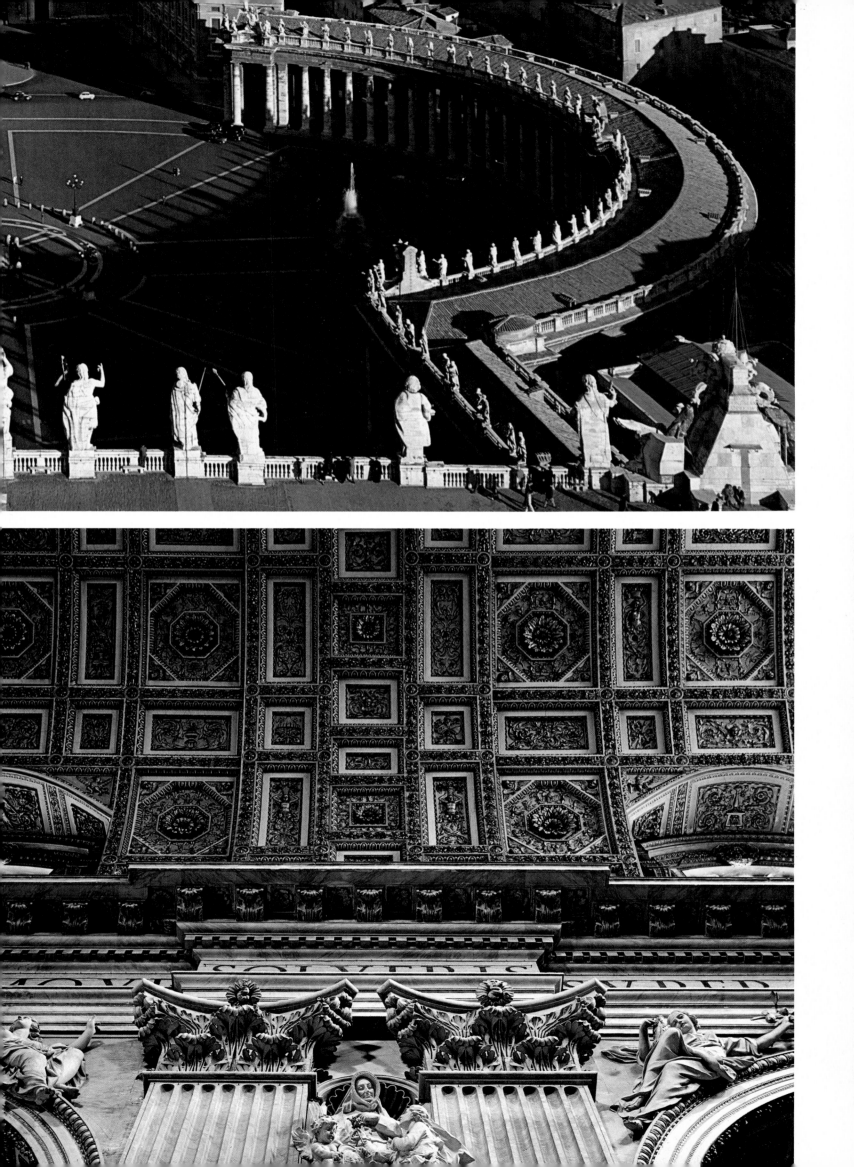

The cathedral of the city and diocese of Rome itself is the Basilica of St. John Lateran. Below, the coat-of-arms of Pope Sixtus V on one of its walls.

SIXTVS V
PONT MAX
ANNO IIII

SANTIAGO DE COMPOSTELA

For medieval people the "package tour", indeed the annual vacation, did not exist. Many people, including those of quite humble status, enjoyed some sort of equivalent by making a pilgrimage to a famous shrine. The custom of the pilgrimage is older than Christianity, and it was accepted by the Catholic Church as early as the 3rd or 4th century. The purpose might be, and usually was, a solem one, but there was no reason why pilgrims should not enjoy themselves along the way, like the characters journeying to St Thomas Becket's shrine in Chaucer's *Canterbury Tales.*

Although God was present in the church—physically present, indeed, in the Eucharist—God was present everywhere, and to most worshippers the most vivid presence in the church was that of the patron saint, who was naturally felt to have a special interest in that particular building. When a church held actual relics of the saint, that interest was held to be powerfully enhanced.

The importance attached to sacred relics, genuine or not, by the medieval Church encouraged the practice of pilgrimage; in fact, many pilgrimages were undertaken for the purpose of securing relics for countries like France, Germany and England, which were not well provided with them. Less ambitious pilgrims brought back tokens of their journey, souvenirs of a kind, to prove they had been there, in the form of a little metal badge which could be worn on the person (there is a good collection of these "pilgrim signs" in the Musée Cluny, Paris). One of the most common survivors is the scallop shell of Santiago (St James) de Compostela, in the north-western corner of Spain. Thanks to the survival of a 12th-century "guidebook" compiled by monks, we can follow the routes of the pilgrims to St James's shrine from all over Europe.

The apostle St James the Great preached Christianity in Roman Spain and, according to tradition, was martyred in Jerusalem about AD 44. His body was returned by more or less miraculous means to Spain, eventually to Compostela. By the 10th century, the shrine of the Apostole became, after Rome, the greatest centre of pilgrimage in Europe.

Romanesque pilgrimage churches, though all different, have a certain similarity—long, barrel—vaulted naves, tall arcades and spacious galleries, with the main artistic emphasis on the shrine at the east end. They tended to acquire subsequent accretions, chapels of this and that,

and the basic Romanesque building at Compostela, which was built between 1075 and 1128, is not easily distinguished. The Portico de la Gloria (completed in 1211), with its statues of the apostles, prophets and elders—St James himself on the central pillar holding a pilgrim's staff—and the powerful Last Judgment in the tympanum, has been called 'one of the greatest glories of Christian art', but more immediately obvious are features such as the stately, towered, Baroque façade that overlooks the main plaza. Within, the figure of St James is enshrined in a tremendous Baroque sanctuary of dully glowing gold. The pilgrims still come.

The lavishly decorated baroque sanctuary of Santiago de Compostela, for centuries past a celebrated place of pilgrimage. St. James is shown in the center of the top of the façade. Right, detail of the door.

The Gothic cathedrals of Spain are, among other things, monuments to the success of Christianity against Islam. In the 10th century, most of the Iberian peninsula except the north-west corner was controlled by the Moors, and it was not until 1492 that Granada, the last Moorish kingdom, was reconquered. The size and scale of the great Spanish cathedrals proclaimed the Church Militant in full array.

At Burgos, the ancient capital of Castile, city of El Cid and, in more recent times, headquarters of General Franco, the note of pride and magnificence is sounded most dramatically. Approached by steep cobbled ramps or long flights of steps, the cathedral holds a commanding position; seen from higher up the slope it dominates a view which stretches across the plains to the distant horizon.

Burgos was begun in 1221 and closely based on French models. Probably, many Frenchmen worked on it; the second master mason, Enrique, who took over in 1243, was possibly

70

French, and the initial building, which was completed very quickly, was bascially in the French High Gothic tradition. But the bones of the structure were largely obscured by the additions of the three centuries following.

The unique effect of Burgos derives from the way its stong, simple, geometric forms are mingled with rich sculptured ornament, notably the decorative spires and pinnacles of which there are no less than 22. Most of these decorative additions were made betwen about 1450 and 1560, and are the work of three generations of the Colonia family. The two magnificent western steeples were built by Hans of Cologne (Juan de Colonia), the Constable's Chapel in the east by his son Simon, and the central tower or lantern (replacing an earlier one) by Simon's son.

The interior is immensely rich and makes an immediate impact of imposing grandeur. That Romantic traveller, Theophile Gautier, who thought Burwos one of the finest cathedrals in the world when he visited it in 1840, spoke of standing in the crossing and looking up at a "giddy abyss of sculptures, arabesques, statues, miniature columns, ribs, lancets and pendentives. One might look at it for two years without seeing everything". He was much intrigued by the ancient coffer alleged to have been the property of El Cid, who filled it with stones and left it as security on a loan from a Jewish usurer on the condition that it should not be opened. "Which proves", as Gautier remarked, "that the usurers of thah time were of a more accomodating nature than those of today". He was puzzled by the purpose of "a great staircase of most beautiful design, whith magnificient carved chimeras" which in fact connects the north transept, built on a higher level owing to the sloping site, with the main church, and he remarked, as many others have since, on the delicate flower-like appearance of the vault of the Constable's Chapel, where the combination of pure geometry and exotic decoration, so typical of Burgos generally, is especially striking.

Burgos Cathedral: general view and façade. Bottom left, the cloister. Below, the Golden Staircase.

SALAMANCA

If one walks south-west from the golden buildings of the Plaza Mayor in Salamanca in the general direction of the Roman bridge, one comes across a sign reading *Cathedrales*. There are indeed two cathedrals in this fabled city. The old cathedral, built mainly in the 12th century, nestles against the southern flank of the new cathedral which, being much larger and higher up the slope, tends to dominate it. The north transept was, in fact, chopped off the old cathedral to make room for the new one, and it is impossible to enter the original building except through the new cathedral. The famous Torre del Gallo, a domed and turreted Romanesque lantern tower, is not seen to the best advantage with the new cathedral looming behind it.

Through less distinguished architecturally, the bold square tower at the west end has an interesting history which cannot easily be guessed from its present appearence. The core of the tower belongs to the old cathedral, as can be seen from the early—albeit restored—frescoes inside. When

the new cathedral was begun in 1512 the tower was refaced in contemporary style, though the old wooden belfry remained. Early in the 18th century the belfry was destroyed by lighning and replaced by a new lantern which, unfortunately, proved too heavy for the existing structure. Some measures were taken to support it, but the earthquake that destroyed Lisbon in 1755 caused cracks in the walls and a dangerous twist in the spire. The bishop hastily vacated his adjacent palace, and experts advised prompt demolition. The citizens, however, were unwilling to knock down their beloved, though rickety tower, and a satisfactory solution was found by Baltasar Derrotón, who encased the whole structure in a strong new coat of stone. The old tower is still there, but no longer visible from the outside.

The basic plan of the new cathedral is rectangular: the transepts do not extend beyond the chapels and the east end is square (no elegant ambulatory, as at Segovia). Although it was not finished until over two hundred years after it was begun, the overall effect is homogeneous, though the decoration of the lantern, the last part to be

built, is slightly out of key with the general Late Gothic atmosphere. A staircase from one of the side chapels leads into the old cathedral, and one passes suddenly from the 16th century to the 12th. Founded three years after the death of El Cid, this solemn building represents a transition phase between Romanesque and Gothic: the nave was intended to be barrel-vaulted, but when that stage was reached, the contemporary master mason opted for quadripartite vaulting, which made it necessary to install the large heads of human beings and lions above the capitals, as support for the ribs. Among other treasures, the old cathedral contains a magnificient 15th-century screen of 55 wooden panels painted with scenes from the life of Christ by Nicolas Florentino, who also painted the Last Judgement in the curve of the apse.

Salamanca, an ancient seat of learning, has two cathedrals; right, the altar and reredos of the older, Romanesque cathedral; above, the far more ornate New Cathedral, seen from the courtyard of its older neighbor.

TOLEDO

An inscription preserved in the cloisters of the cathedral in Toledo records the dedication of a Visigothic church to Our Lady in 589. It is possible that this church was the same as that of the four early Toledan bishops who were canonized, one of them said to have been a disciple of St Paul. Legend also says that the site was recommended by St James himself and the church built while the Virgin Mary was still alive. (She was so gratified that she is said to have visited the church in 666, and the stone altar table where she stood can still be seen in the Capilla de la Descensión.) The church became a mosque in the 8th century and was demolished by St Ferdinand (Ferdinand III of Castile) who founded the present cathedral in 1227.

Toledo is an ancient city—founded by Herakles according to one legend—and its early history is largely bound up with the history of the Church in Spain. It was the scene of many early Church councils and the long struggle between Spanish Catholicism and Arianism was fought out here. The archbishop of Toledo is still recognised as the primate of Spain, but the city declined in importance in the 16th century after the revolt of the Comuneros and the decision of Philip II to make his capital at Madrid. Its former importance and subsequent decline accounts for the medieval appearance that Toledo retains.

Despite various historical outrages, such as despoliation by the French during the Peninsula

War, the cathedral remains one of the finest and richest in Spain. A broad, five-aisled church somewhat similar to Bourges in plan (though wider), it was constructed largely between the 13th and 16th centuries, and the basic Gothic design is augmented by Renaissance and Baroque features. The exterior is less extravagant than that of Burgos, but sturdy and solid, "clothed in russet tones, the colour of a browning roast or of a skin tanned like that of a pilgrim from Palestine". The interior is much more elaborately sculptured, and the great space is imposing. The central nave is high, the vault supported by 88 piers, each made up of sixteen embracing columns ; but the great

Toledo Cathedral is quite as imposing as the city's famous Alcazar. Opposite page, overall view and detail of the tower. Left, the façade. Above and below, the cloister.

width of the building makes it seem less. The light that filturs through the emerald, sapphire and ruby tones of the stained-glass windows is soft and mysterious ; vast gilded altarpieces, superbly carved wooden choir stalls, alabaster tombs and figures, all add to the atmosphere of solemn luxury. Among other treasures, the cathedral treasury contains a famous silver-gilt monstrance, one of the most remarkable pieces of Spanish medieval art (but with some Renaissance additions), which is still carried in procession through the streets. There are many chapels, mostly of comparatively late date, including the frescoed Mozarabic Chapel, commemorating the rites of those Chistians who remained in Toledo throughout the Moorish period. The rites, which differ from the Latin rites in several respects, are still celebrated in Toledo cathedral and in only two other churches.

SEGOVIA

"... In the distance", wrote Ortega y Gasset, "the cathedral of Segovia sails ahead amid the yellow corn, like a huge mysterious liner which overwhelms the rest of the town by its bulk... [It] seems by some optical illusion to be cleaving the harvest field with its apse as it moves forward. Between its flying buttresses we catch glimpses of blue sky, as we glimpse the sky through the stays and rigging of a ship".

If possible, one should approch Segovia from the north on an autumn evening, to catch the golden glow of the cathedral in the setting sun. The skyline of the city, backed here and there by the smooth slopes of the Sierra de Guadarrama and commanded by the great, towered cathedral, will look familiar even to those who have never visited the city before, because as many an amateur water-colourist and many a Spanish travel poster have procalimed, there is something essentially Spanish about the whole scene of stone and whitewashed houses, huge stone church, towers and pinnacles of the Alcázar, and the backrop of distant hills.

The old cathedral, near the Alcázar, had been seriously damaged in 1520 during the Revolt of the Comuneros, when Segovia was unsuccessfully besieged by royalist forces, and construction of the present cathedral began in 1525. The architect was Juan Gil de Hontañón, who had been working at Salamanca since 1513, and the plan of Segovia closely resembled the earlier cathedral. Most of the work was completed by his

son, Rodrigo, who died in 1577 (he is commemorated by a stone tablet in the cloisters), and Segovia cathedral is the last monumental example of the great age of Spanish building, in which the Gothic style mingled with the new influences of the Renaissance. Moreover, thanks to its speed of construction, Segovia, like Salisbury in England, is architecturally consistent in style. It does contain some furnishings from the old cathedral, including the choir stalls and the figure of the *Virgen del Perdón,* inside the main west door.

The siting of the cathedral makes the most of its great size (it is one of the largest in Spain), but the building is light and graceful. The Late Gothic style of Spain, with its plateresque (i.e. like the work of a silversmith) decoration is too florid for some tastes, but the exterior of Segovia is for the most part comparatively plain. There is little external sculpture and the main entrance in the west, often the object of the most extravagant adornment, is at Segovia simple and restrained. The great tower, some 16 metres square and nearly 90 metres high, can be climbed by the vigorous (306 steps, the guides say), who are repaid for their effot by a marvellous view.

Among the rich treasures and ornaments of the cathedral are ancient manuscripts, Gobelin tapestries, and a number of tombs.

Segovia: overall view of the cathedral, and decorative work on the outside of the choir. Above: a low-relief depicting St. Martin cutting his cloak.

SEVILLE

The lively, picturesque life of the streets of Seville has often been commemorated in the arts, not least by composers of opera (Rossini's *Barbiere di Siviglia,* Mozart's *Figaro,* Bizet's *Carmen),* and a mixture of people from the surrounding country, heavily spiced by tourists, still flock to the bull fights, carnivals and festivals of the city. Traditional customs—and costumes—can still be seen. Nowhere in Europe are the great religious festivals celebrated with so much splendour, and Holy Week in Seville has long been a famous occasion. At Corpus Christi the choir boys of the cathedral perform a curious, solemn dance with castanets before the High Altar, and the cathedral contains images and other objects which are traditionally carried in procession through the streets, among them the great silver monstrance, nearly four metres high, made by Juan de Arfe in the 16th century.

The cathedral, Santa Maria de la Sede, is an extraordinary building by any standards. The 15th-century builders are said to have remarked that anyone looking at the finished building would be so struck by its size and shape that he would think them mad. That sounds like a sure recipe for failure, but in fact the grandiose project was successfully completed in the course of little more than one hundred years (1402-1520). Visitors today, though certainly impressed, are not likely to doubt the sanity of the builders, and as it happens the shape and even the size of the building are not easily discerned. Amid the jumble of alleys and surrounding buildings, it is impossible to get a clear overall view: in this, as in many other cases, a helicopter would be handy.

The cathedral of Seville is generally agreed to be the largest medieval church in Europe. Roughly rectangular in shape, it measures approximately 130 by 80 metres; including the patio, it occupies about 18,000 square metres. The height of the crossing is 56 metres, of the nave vault 40 metres. The unusual shape and size are dictated by the fact that it was erected on the situ of a mosque. The campanile, known as the Giralda (90 metres), which stands at the northeast corner, was originally a minaret and it is still covered with Moorish decoration below the belfry. The general exterior appearance is rather shapeless, owing to later additions (including the Baroque parish church north of the cathedral) and to the absence, apart from the Giralda, of a marked silhouette. There is some resemblance to Milan cathedral, though Seville is less fanciful.

The huge space of the interior, with 32 vast clustered piers and over seventy windows, is augmented by rich objects of art, most notably the Late Gothic screen of gilded wood showing incidents from the life of Christ. There are paintings by many Spanish masters, fine Renaissance carvings and metalwork, magnificent tombs and, not least, the wooden image of the Virgin (with movable arms and hair of spun gold) presented by St Louis to St Ferdinand in the 13th century.

Seville: the cathedral, near the Giralda. Right, the organ and the transept. Left, the Chapter House.

GUARDA

The Portuguese town of Guarda which, lying at an altitude of almost 1,000 metres above sea level, is the highest town in the country, is not often visited by tourists despite its own attractions and those of the surrounding district. Overlooking the sheep-dotted slopes of the Serra do Estrêla and the fertile valley of the River Côa, it is a breezy, sometimes chilly place which has a reputation for healthful air; the hospital, with its attractive courtyard, was built as a sanatarium for sufferers from tuberculosis.

The city was founded in the 12th century on the site of a Roman fort by Sancho I, but it looks as if it has been there even longer. Its rough granite walls seem to have grown out of the soil. There are some attractive houses, streets lined with jumbled arcades, and many other picturesque details but, apart from a Baroque church and castle ruins, there is only one great building in the town. That is a monument sufficient for many more pretentious places, the Sé or cathedral.

As the name implies, the original purpose of Guarda was defence : along with Celorico and Trancoso it formed part of the north-eastern defensive system against the Moors. After the Moors had gone, Guarda continued to keep watch on the Spanish frontier, 40 km away, and according to legend there is, among the cathedral's lively array of gargoyles, on which, looking directly towards Spain, makes a markedly offensive gesture. Perhaps there was once; it does not appear to be there now.

The gargoyles are not the only aspect of Guarda cathedral which suggest French influence. The building, founded about 1390 and built mainly in the 15th and early 16th centuries, imitated the well-known monastic church of Batalha, which in turn was strongly influenced by French and Norman design. Guarda, however, was built not of warm, embracing limestone but of harsh, dark granite, which gives it an appearance, appropriate to the historical function of the city, of hard, uncompromising power. The west façade, its ornate, almost Baroque portal somewhat at odds with the simplicity of the rest, looks as if it could withstand the fiercest siege. Yet the general design is both rich and complicated, and the characteristically florid furnishings in the Portuguese Late Gothic style known as Manueline (after King Manuel I, 1495-1521) contribute a certain nationalistic grandeur. As we look at the cathedral of Guarda, we remember that 15th-century Portugal was a very remarkable country which, despite a tiny population, was leading the way in the European discovery of other continents, with incalculable effects on world history.

The interior dimensions of the cathedral are impressive: the long, high nave is divided from the aisles by rectangular columns, but the pair of columns at the crossing are fashioned in cable-twist style, a rather surprising effect though a well known Manueline device, found elsewhere in this cathedral. The stone altarpiece, the richly decorated door of the sacristy, and the delicate Renaissance glass of the transepts are among the most cherished works of the cathedral.

The most remarkable cathedral in Portugal is situated in Guarda. Above, side view. Left, the sanctuary, surrounded by the rooftops of the small town, and its façade.

MOSCOW

An American tourist in Red Square, setting eyes on the cathedral of St Basil (Vasili) for the first time, exclaimed in wonder, "Disneyland!" The reaction is not easily excusable, although there is undoubtedly something incongruous in the spectacle of tanks, missiles and grim-faced soldiers marching past this joyful building. Yet St Basil's is a military symbol in its way.

The name of Ivan the Terrible sounds a dreadful note in popular mythology, and for once a legendary reputation seems to be no great exaggeration of historical facts. There is something not unappealing, in a macabre way, about a ruler who ordered an elephant to be chopped to bits because it refused to bow to him, but Ivan's personality defects, if that is what they can be called, brought horror, disaster and death to his people on an unprecedented scale.

Before his tenuous grasp on reality finally gave way, Ivan was a great conqueror, and it was to celebrate his conquests over the Tatars that Pokrovsky cathedral, better known as St Basil's, was built. A revolutionary building in its day, it was founded in 1554 and completed in 1679; it proclaims the triumphs of Russian nationalism and the Orthodox Church. The prime mover, if not Ivan himself, was probably the Metropolitan Makarii, himself a painter and patron of the arts. It consists basically of eight separate chapels, each dedicated to a saint whose holiday coincided with one of Ivan's battles, clustering around a central tower to which they are linked by passages. Each unit is treated independently: all eight bulb-shaped domes have a different design, suggesting

a basket of tropical fruit, yet the building has an undeniable unity. The effect is certainly exotic, too rich for the taste of many observers who perhaps are not aware that the original building was whitewashed: the ornate polychrome decoration which accounts for the alleged Disneyland effect was added in the 18th century. The cathedral also required restoration in the 19th century after it had been plundered by the French.

Few of the finest buildings of the period in Moscow were built by Muscovites. When Ivan III began the reconstruction of the Kremlin at the end of the 15th century he was forced to seek help from Paskov after the rebuilt Cathedral of the Dormition (the coronation church of the tsars) had collapsed on reaching the height of the vaults. Subsequently the Kremlin project was largely completed by Italian architects, who were first compelled to study the principles of Byzantine architecture. But St Basil's, the most famous of the churches of the tsars, is, despite the novelty of its design, a thoroughly Russian building, built by Russian craftsmen and owing much to traditional Russian architecture in wood. The tent-shaped silhouette, and variations on it, seen in St Basil's and elsewhere, is derived from this tradition, in which Russian architects were more expert than they were in stone. St Basil's itself was to inspire many later churches, like the great Cathedral of the Resurrection in Leningrad begun in 1883.

Above: the first cathedral of Moscow. Right, St. Basil's Cathedral, decorative detail and its astonishing belltowers.

In 989 Vladimir, prince of the old Russian state of Kiev, returned from a campaign in the south a converted Christian. He brought with him Byzantine icons, crosses and other sacred items, and he ordered the pagan idols of Kiev to be thrown into the river where, a few days later, his obedient people repaired to be baptised. This episode marks the beginning of the Christian Middle Ages of Russia, in which Byzantine art and the Orthodox Church combined to form the major theme of Russian culture.

The earliest churches of Kiev have not survived: we do know that they were generally Byzantine in character, on the plan of a Greek cross with one large and several subsidiary domes. The cathedral of S. Sophia, begun in 1037, is probably the earliest surviving building, though from the outside it is difficult to detect any evidence of its original appearance; it is merely a fine example of Ukrainian Baroque.

S. Sophia was designed to be a much grander building than its immediate predecessors, rivalling S. Sophia in Constantinople. It had five aisles, instead of the usual three, and no less than thirteen domes, set in tiers like an ascending pyramid with the great central dome, the symbol of Christ topped by a cross, crowning all. Such a dazzling domical display had not been seen before anywhere in the Byzantine world. The exterior was banded with alternating horizontal courses of brick and pinkish mortar, though there is little to be seen of this effect now.

Inside, one's first impression is of the skill with which the Byzantine architects handled the admission of daylight. The large central area is well illuminated while the aisles recede into gloom. The chief decorative features are frescoes and mosaics, which in Orthodox Christianity played much the same role as stained glass and sculpture in Roman Catholic Churches. S. Sophia is dominated by the impressive, indeed forbidding, mosaic of Christ Pantocrator ("universal ruler") in the central dome, which is illuminated by the windows immediately below. Three of the four angels' heads which surround the circular picture were restored in oil paint in the 19th century, but they are not so easily distinguished from the one surviving 11th-century head as one might expect. Another enormous figure, the Virgin Orans ("praying") is placed in the curve of the sanctuary, above a scene of the Eucharist. The painstaking skill that the unknown Byzantine masters put into their work becomes more clearly apparent on close examination of the Kiev mosaics. For example, someone almost equally painstaking has counted the glass cubes used in certain sections of the last-mentioned mosaic. In a figure of an apostle appearing in the Eucharist scene the face — the most detailed part of the design — contains approximatuly 400 cubes per square decimeter. By contrast the background, where less detail is required, contains about 150 cubes per square decimeter.

The Cathedral of Saint Sophia, Kiev. Right, ornamental detail from the interior of the Dome of the Trinity.

ISTANBUL

Early in the reign of Justinian, the greatest of the East Roman emperors, a revolt broke out in Constantinople in the course of which several of the chief buildings were destroyed. Among the casualties was the Church of Divine Wisdom, Hagia Sophia, which was both the cathedral church of Constantinople and the palace church of the emperor. Prestige demanded that it be rapidly replaced, and that the new church should be a building of such magnificence it would astound all who entered it. Justinian entrusted the task to Anthemius of Tralles and his nephew Isidorus of Miletus; between 532 and 537 they built what is universally regarded as the supreme masterpiece of Byzantine architecture.

The chief distinguishing feature of Byzantine architecture was the adoption of the dome in the building of churches. A secondary characteristic was the use of brick as the main building material. Now, the Romans had built domes, and

they had also used bricks (though they did not build brick domes). But the Pantheon, the most famous Roman domed building, had circular walls, and it is not difficult to build a large dome on a circular wall providing the latter is thick enough. It is a different matter to raise a dome on a square. The Byzantines overcame the problem at a remarkably early period by the device of the pendentive — a concave, triangular section with the point at the right angle of two walls or arches, rising to form a quarter circle at the height of the arches. Such a structure transmits the weight of the dome evenly to the main supports at the four corners. Further buttressing can be provided in a number of ways.

At Hagia Sophia, the great brick dome, which has the same diameter as the Pantheon

(about 29 metres) was buttressed by two half-domes of the same diameter on the east and west (the main axis, since the basilican nave is twice as long as it is wide). To the north and south, a wall of columns was strengthened by enormous interior buttresses. These in fact proved insufficiently strong: an earthquake brought down the dome in 588, and it had to be rebuilt again in 989.

The exterior of Hagia Sophia, with its flanking minarets erected by the Turks, is much

Top left, the Cathedral of Hagia Sophia, Istanbul, seen from the Blue Mosque, with the Bosphorus in the background. Above, the interior and, bottom left, partial view of the great cupola. Right, mosaic.

less impressive than the interior (it suffers slightly from an unfortunate resemblance to cinemas of the 1930s). Inside, the effect is stunning. One's first impression is of a huge airy space, with the shallow dome hovering "as if suspended by a chain from heaven" — an effect greatly assisted by the forty small windows let into the lower part of the dome. The effect in detail is of extreme delicacy, with glittering mosaics, glowing coloured marbles and intricately carved capitals (some bearing Justinian's monogram). According to legend, when Justinian first stepped into the finished building he exclaimed, "Solomon, I have triumphed over you!" It is a measure of his triumph that this Christian church was the model for many Turkish mosques after the conquest of 1453.

NEW YORK

New York, they say, has everything. Perhaps not everything, but it does, surprisingly, have Gothic cathedrals. As one would expect, they are among the largest such buildings anywhere; in fact the Protestant cathedral of St John the Divine is claimed to be second only to St Peter's, Rome, as the largest church in the world. (These figures mean little, however; it depends on how the measurements are made, and the number of cathedrals which are said by guidebooks to be among the six largest must be at least twenty!) St John's, with Central Park to the south and Harlem to the north, covers a site of nearly five hectares and should seat a congregation of 15,000. It was begun in 1892; the original Romanesque design was scrapped in favour of Gothic after the deaths of the original architects in 1911. In the medieval manner, it has been built piece by piece as money becomes available and it is unlikely to be finished before the end of the century. Standing inside the building today, one is overwhelmed by the sheer size of every unit.

The Roman Catholic cathedral of St Patrick stands in mid-Manhattan, its spires (53 metres high) completely dwarfed by the immense towers of Rockefeller Center and other office skyscrapers. The view was different when the cathedral was built, but cynics regard the present situation as perfectly symbolic of the ascendancy of the material over the spiritual world.

It is the ambition of every young New York Irishman and woman to be married in St Pat's. Erected entirely with locally raised funds, it can be regarded as a sign of the achievement of social equality by the Irish population, for the antagonism towards Irish immigrants in the United States in the early 19th century was largely due to their religion, and the original St Patrick's in downtown Manhattan (still standing but now a parish church) was attacked by mobs on several occasions.

There are nearly four million Catholics in New York City, a great many of whom do not speak English. At St Patrick's, confessions can be heard in several languages; there is also a special confessional for the deaf mute.

James Renwick, scion of a brilliant family of engineers, was selected to design the new cathedral in 1853 (he appears in a window of the south transept). An enthusiast for the Gothic Revival in architecture (though later, when designing opulent villas for the New York social set, he became more eclectic), Renwick planned a fusion of French, German and English Gothic, but his plans were much altered during construction; the final result is predominantly French in effect, with a suggestion of Cologne. The building was complete by 1879 except for the spires (1887) and the Lady Chapel (1906). The granite cathedral has a wood and plaster vault and, as a result, flying buttresses were unnecessary to support the vault and were therefore omitted.

A short distance apart on Fifth Avenue in New York: St. Patrick's Cathedral (left), Catholic, a surprising sight among the tower blocks and seen from Rockefeller Center— and the Episcopalian Cathedral of St.John the Divine (above). Both are in the neo-Gothic style. Right, the baptistry, St. John's.

Among the devout Christians of Mexico, religion is somehow a more intimate affair than it is in many European countries. The Mexicans embraced Christianity with an eagerness very gratifying to the early Spanish missionaries, though it must be said that the mass baptisms reported by the friars sound a little doubtful; moreover, aspects of the old pagan religion, merging with Christian ideas, have proved very vigorous. In recent times anticlericalism has ensured that the priests have played a less dominant role than in earlier times, and when the novelist Graham Greene visited Mexico in 1938 he reported that he could find only five hundred priests in the whole country actually carrying out their pastoral duties. No doubt that assisted the development of the familiar relationship apparent between ordinary people and the saints to whom they pray. From superficial appearances, certainly, the new basilica of the Virgin of Guadelupe is a more popular shrine than the mighty symbol of Spanish colonialism that dominates the vast Zócalo (Plaza de la Constitución).

The dimensions of the cathedral are imposing: length 118 metres, width 54 metres, height (of

the western towers) 62 metres. Standing on the site of an Aztec temple, it is basically a typical example of the Spanish colonial Baroque as employed in many other Mexican cathedrals, but more restrained than most. Consecrated in 1656, its construction had commenced nearly a century earlier, and it was not completed for another century and a half. Owing to this long period of construction, it displays in its architecture and decoration features of virtually all the styles of Spanish colonial art. Some of the vaulting is Gothic, while each bay of the side aisles is domed. The western façade is mainly Neo-Classical, with white marble statues and other details framed against the warm brown limestone of the building. This is largely the work of the Creole architect José Ortiz de Castro (who deserves to be better known) and dates from the late 18th century, but some of the decorative work, plus the lantern and dome, was designed by Manuel Tolsa of Valencia early in the 19th century. It is the view of the cathedral from the west, with the benefit of the open space of the Zócalo in front, that is most

rewarding. It is particularly dramatic when artificially illuminated by night.

The most famous work of art in the metropolitan cathedral is undoubtedly the altarpiece in the Chapel of the Three Kings, an incredibly ornate creation of gilded columns, which almost disappear beneath the wealth of ornament and polychrome statuary. It was made between 1718 and 1737 by Jerónimo de Balbas, and is a splendid example of that extreme manifestation of the Baroque style of Castile known as Churrigueresque (after the Churriguera brothers) which is evident on a larger scale in the adjacent Sagrario Metropolitano.

The Cathedral, Mexico City, with its monumental façade (right), its lavish gilt-decorated interior (above) and the extremely ornate style of its doors (left), is a true symbol of the fabled riches of the New World, coupled with the most traditional Spanish mysticism.

BRASILIA

The city of Brasilia is a gesture, a large-minded symbol of Brazil's confidence in its vast, unexploited – in places almost unexplored – hinterland and, correspondingly, of the national determination to break away from the influence of countries overseas. (Even now, 80 per cent of Brazil's 120 million people live within 80 kilometres of the coast.) The idea of moving the capital into the interior was canvassed as long ago as 1808 and was enshrined in the constitution of

1889, but it was not until 1956 that a site was chosen and construction begun. Within three years a habitable city was created "on the very spot", as one of the guidebooks puts it, "where once the jaguar roared". Despite the doubling of their salaries, civil servants who were told they must forsake their homes in the jolly city of Rio de Janeiro to start a new life in the wilderness nearly 1,000 kilometres away were not pleased, and Brasilia got off to a poor start. One of the kinder verdicts on the project was "inspired lunacy" and, to this day, people who have never

been to Brasilia regard it vaguely as a place built at vast expense where nobody wants to live. The expense cannot be denied, but Brasilia no longer gives an impression of a half-deserted Utopia, a mirage on the plains.

The most modern city in the world had the advantage of major buildings designed by a great contemporary architect, Oscar Niemeyer. No concessions were made either to cost or to local technical capacity (when asked how much the Alvorada Palace had cost, Niemeyer shrugged, "I do not know. How should I know?"). Not all the

tower blocks of Brasilia are pleasing, but Niemeyer's cathedral is a work of art, in which sophisticated engineering techniques are employed to create what looks like a gigantic piece of sculpture rather than a building. Niemeyer, though a Brazilian, was not a Christian, and his curious, hump-backed church at Pampulha, Belo Horizonte, was refused consecration by the bishop partly because of the architect's known Communist sympathies. Delays also attended the building of the cathedral, which had progressed far enough for the city's inaugural Mass to be celebrated there in 1960 but thereafter advanced at creeping pace.

The cathedral takes the form of a crown of thorns, fashioned from sixteen curved, hollow,

After so many manifestations of the fervor of centuries past in the old nations of Europe, Brasilia Cathedral provides a strikingly modern and artistic rendering of the yearning for spiritual elevation common to man of all periods.

concrete ribs some thirty metres high. Others have likened it to hands raised in prayer. The nave is below ground and is entered by the darkened Passage of Reflection, from which one emerges into the light and airy space of the circular nave, which is capable of holding 4,000 people. The interior is generally austere, and the eye is drawn to the marble High Altar and the statue of St Puter suspended from the roof. The glass panels of the roof reflect the water in a surrounding pool, which in turn magically reflects shimmering images of nearby buildings.

TOKYO

During the 19th and 20th centuries a considerable number of new cathedrals have been built, and in some ways the challenge is still as great as it was for the architects of medieval Europe. During the 19th century, church architecture remained largely traditional, with the Gothic style predominating, especially in large cathedrals like St John the Divine in New York or the recently completed Anglican cathedral in Liverpool. The 20th century has witnessed radical departures in architecture as in other arts, and they have affected ecclesiastical building no less than others.

The two outstanding cathedrals of recent times were both designed by non-believers —

Oscar Niemeyer in Brasilia and Kenzo Tange in Tokyo. The great Japanese architect, an immensely influential teacher and writer as well as a world-famous designer of public buildings, whose Olympic Stadium showed him to be among the most daring of contemporary architects, has produced a building which combines with brilliant success revolutionary concepts of structure with traditional symbolic form. For St Mary's cathedral, which swoops up from among the crowded, low rise houses in the Bunkyo district of Tokyo like a great silver bird, is built on the plan of a Latin cross.

The cathedral has no "walls" or "roof" in the conventional sense. Vast, shimmering sails or "shells", clad in ribbed stainless steel, rise from the cruciform ground plan in sweeping double

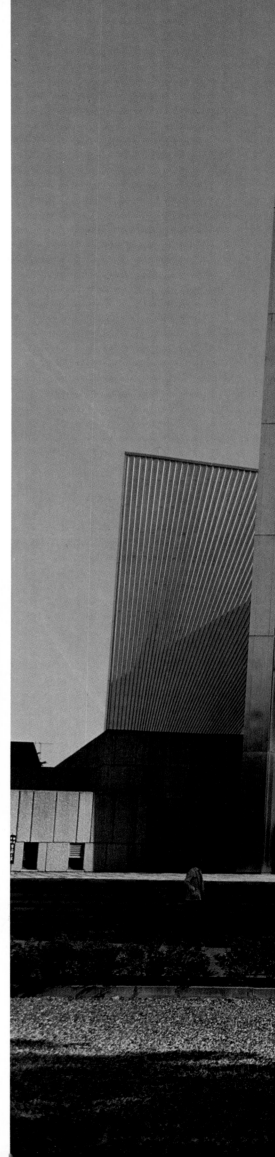

curves to another, much narrower cross at the top, which is formed of skylight ribbons running the whole length of each arm, interspersed with crossbeams bracing the shells. The ribbons rise upwards from the centre and, when they reach the four peaks at the ends of the arms, they descend as windows in straight lines to the ground.

The cathedral was built in 1961-64 to replace an earlier building, destroyed during the Second World War. Certain restrictions were placed on the plan by the shape of the site, though no one would guess that Tange's winning design in the competition for the new cathedral was affected by such petty inconveniences. At St Mary's, Tange has taken the traditional Gothic form and made it abstract, an effect accentuated by the lack of sculpture and by the tapering concrete needle of the campanile, standing sixty metres high, well apart from the main building, from which one expects to hear electronic music

rather than bells.

The entrances are in two low annexes (equivalent to medieval aisles) flanking the nave, which also contains chapels. Inside, where the light is filtered through louvres on the skylights, the soaring concrete shells (still bearing the marks of the shuttering in the manner popularised by Le Corbusier) produce initially a slight feeling of disorientation, but one swiftly senses the subtle essence of the building and is lost in admiration at the austere, upward-sweeping forms which recall the ideals of the great cathedral builders of the Middle Ages.

St. Mary's Cathedral, Tokyo, is a new example of the powerful, sweeping perspectives to be encountered in modern religious architecture.